KINGS and QUEENS of ENGLAND

ALAN PALMER

octopus

First published in 1976 in Great Britain by
Octopus Books Limited, 59 Grosvenor Street,
London W.1.

This book was devised and produced by
George Weidenfeld and Nicolson Limited

Designed by Marion Neville
Picture editor Julia Brown
House editor Esther Jagger

Distributed in USA by Crescent Books
a division of Crown Publisher's, Inc.
One Park Avenue,
New York, N.Y. 10016

Produced by Mandarin Publishers Limited
22a Westlands Road, Quarry Bay, Hong Kong,
Printed in Hong Kong.

Contents

1 Norman Yoke 1066~1164

page 8

2 Power of the Throne 1164~1272

page 26

6 Stuart Catastrophe 1603~1688

page 88

7 Protestant Establishment 1688~1820

page 104

3 Three Edwards
1272~1377

4 Struggle for the Throne
1377~1485

5 Tudor Magnificence
1485~1603

8 Expansion and Prosperity
1820~1901

9 The People's Kings
1901~1952

Epilogue The New Elizabethans

1
Norman Yoke 1066~1164

O N Christmas Day 1066 Duke William of Normandy rode to Westminster Abbey for his coronation as ruler of England. Outside the church, consecrated the previous December, a guard of Norman knights sat uneasily astride their mounts. Only ten weeks previously they had been locked in battle against the thegns and housecarls of the English army north of Hastings. Now, although a group of eminent Londoners had invited the victorious William to ascend the English throne, the knights did not trust their lord's new subjects, whose language neither they nor William himself could speak or understand. Suddenly, as the ceremony reached its climax, they heard a disturbance within the abbey: Archbishop Ealdred of York was inviting the people to

affirm their recognition of William's sovereignty. They assumed that the shouts of acclamation, in English, were treacherous calls to rise against the invader. In panic they set fire to the surrounding buildings. William I was thus consecrated, crowned and enthroned in December half-light, with tongues of flame luridly lapping the stone walls of the abbey. It was an apt beginning to a reign in which respect for the Church and its traditions alone mitigated the brutal fact of military domination.

When he ascended the English throne William the Conqueror was about forty, a thick-set man of medium height. For more than twenty years he had devoted his energies to safeguarding the duchy of Normandy, of which he had become titular ruler as a child. Internal revolts, the

LEFT William the Conqueror, a detail from the Bayeux Tapestry.

OPPOSITE Caen Abbey in Normandy, founded by William's wife Matilda.

Ego Willms cognoie Bastard⁹ Rex Anglie do ⁊
⁊ concedo tibi Nepoti meo Alano Britanñe Comiti
⁊ hredibꝯ tuis inꝑⁿ omñes villas ⁊ tras que
nuꝑ fuerut Comitis Edwyni in Eboꝶcsħ
⁊ cu feodis ꝓhliti ⁊ eodñs ⁊ aliis libeꝶt
⁊ ꝯuetudiꝯ ita libe ⁊ honorifice sicut idꝰ
Edwin̄ ea tenuit. Dat in obsione cozam
Ciuitate Ebor.

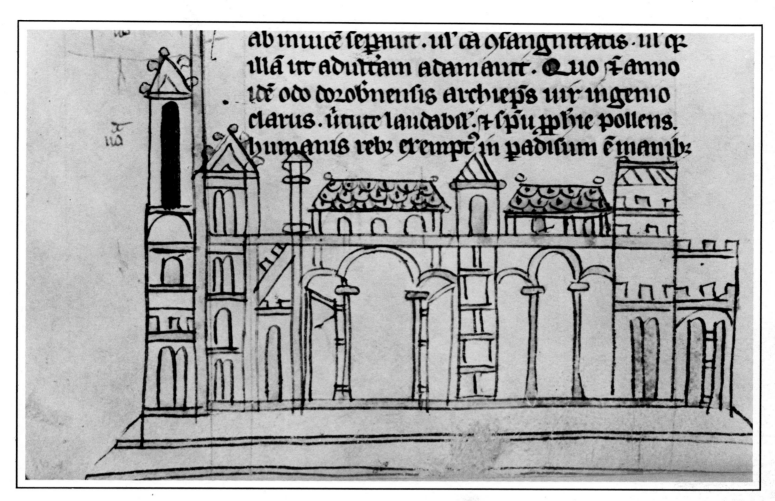

ab inuice sepmir. ul' ca osangiutratis. ul' ex
illa ur adulrerin adam auur. Quo fanno
ide oco corobnensis archieps ur ingenio
clarus. urure laudabit'. + spu ppine pollens.
humanis reb? exempr? in padisum e manib?

ABOVE Westminster Abbey,
where William I was crowned
on Christmas Day, 1066.

OPPOSITE William presenting a
charter to his nephew Alan.

private wars of well-armed retainers, and threats to his borders from the King of France and the Count of Anjou made William a seasoned campaigner. He was distinguished both as a tactical cavalry commander and, more unusually, as a long-term strategist who was able to organize and maintain troops on a large scale. His qualities of leadership, together with his genuine respect for the Church, impressed his distant cousin, King Edward the Confessor, whom he visited in England fourteen years before the battle of Hastings. It is probable that the saintly and childless Edward promised William the English succession, and certainly Norman influence was strong at Edward's Court. The English monarchy did not, as yet, rest on any hereditary principle and none of the claimants of Anglo-Saxon or Danish royal descent were sufficiently powerful to unify the different elements of the nation. But Edward was not entitled to decide who was to succeed him. There were other contenders more readily acceptable to the English magnates than the masterful ruler of Normandy. Chief among these contenders was Harold, the brother of Edward the Confessor's wife, a soldier who had fought alongside Duke William in Brittany and taken an oath of loyalty to him. Harold became King of England in the opening week of the year 1066, only to perish in battle near Hastings ten months later.

OPPOSITE The Normans were master builders and brought with them a new type of architecture. Characteristic round-topped Norman arches are much in evidence in the north transept of Winchester Cathedral.

RIGHT Later Norman architecture shows the more decorative but still round-topped arch of the Romanesque style. Iffley Church, Oxford-shire.

William at first organized England as he had organized his duchy. He travelled through the country, establishing garrisons in the principal towns and building castles to overawe his subjects. Theoretically he claimed to be restoring the good laws of Edward the Confessor's reign, menaced by Harold and the usurping Earls of the old English kingdom. But in practice the English were gradually deprived of their landed possessions, excluded from administrative office, and forced to pay heavy taxes and communal fines. Serious rebellions in 1069 finally destroyed any attempt to establish genuine Anglo-Norman partnership in government. Twenty years after the battle of Hastings there were only two English-born barons owning estates by grace of King William, one in the county of Warwick, the other near Lincoln. The King's authority in civil administration was represented by the sheriffs, all-powerful servants of the sovereign within their particular counties. The baronial magnates, holding lands in return for heavy military obligations, were a potential danger to a weak ruler, but not to William himself. He saw to it that their possessions were scattered far and wide, so as to prevent them from raising any particular geographical region in revolt against him. The most serious threat came always from the north, partly because of the possibility of a Scandinavian invasion, and William imposed a stern feudal yoke on Cheshire, Durham and Yorkshire. It was in those counties, and in the northern Midlands, that the Norman conquest seemed most cruel. By 'harrying the north' in 1069 the Norman army left a trail of scorched earth to deter resistance in this crucial frontier zone for many generations. The guerrilla activities of Hereward in the Isle of Ely never threatened the Conqueror's hold on his kingdom but they were a military embarrassment to William who was forced personally to conduct siege operations

Continued on pg 16

13

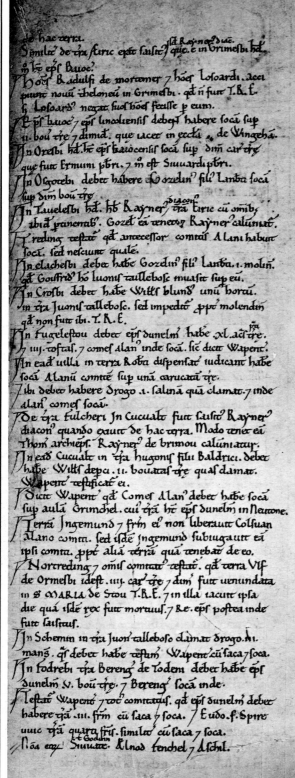

ABOVE Monks and fishermen played an important part in the economy of Domesday England. From a parchment illustrating the life of a twelfth-century anchorite.

LEFT A page from Domesday Book, the monumental survey of England carried out on William I's instructions in 1086.

In the museum of the Public Record Office at Chancery Lane in London there are two massive volumes of manuscript on show to visitors. These form the complete transcribed text of the survey of the English shires ordered by William I at Christmas 1085 and carried out by royal commissioners who travelled through the country in 1086. So detailed was the information recorded that it was regarded as legal testimony against which there could be no appeal until the end of the world. Hence the nickname given by contemporaries – Domesday Book.

The book was primarily, but not exclusively, a large-scale tax return. It was therefore unpopular. An Anglo-Saxon chronicler complained of Norman interference: 'So precisely did [King William] order the survey to be carried out that there was scarcely a hide, a rood of land, nor – it is shameful to relate although he thought it not shameful to do – was there an ox, cow or swine not set down in the writ.' The kingdom was divided into a number of circuits (probably nine) and commissioners collected information from sworn juries of local inhabitants, whether racially English or Norman in origin. The effect of this survey was to provide the government of England with a unique written record of who owned 'the woods, pastures and meadows' of England. If such information was valuable in assessing taxation, it became of even greater value as a written basis for the law of ownership and property. For that reason it was 'edited' by the royal scribes so as to appear under the names of feudal magnates.

The picture of England conjured up by Domesday is a land of extensive royal forests and of open fields, with a few townships in forest clearings or at river-crossings. There are no compact farms and hedgerows as in later times. The open fields were divided into strips of round-backed ridges separated from one another by ploughed furrows, which carried away the water. Many settlements were protected by castles, often little more than mounds. The ridge and furrow effect of the fields, and the fortified earthworks, sometimes survive today, archaeological evidence amplifying the information of Domesday Book.

Domesday England was a feudal kingdom in which 'every man had a lord', to whom he rendered service. Although the King was overlord of the realm, the tenant who worked the fields might hold his land from a baron, a bishop or the abbot of a monastery. The lord's lands were scattered over the shires just as the peasants' strips were scattered over the open fields. The greater Norman barons had lands on both sides of the Channel; and so indeed did thirty of the greater abbeys. Without a census on the scale of Domesday it would have been impossible for the king's administrators to impose order and uniformity on a conquered land thus parcelled out among a largely alien nobility.

ABOVE Norman influence in the south of England was understandably strong. Sompting Church, Sussex.

LEFT Chepstow Castle on the Welsh border, a Norman stronghold indicating the extent of the invaders' penetration into Britain.

:VENIT:ADPA LATIÛ SVÛ

ABOVE Harold and William in conversation, a scene from the Bayeux Tapestry.

against Ely by land and water throughout the summer of 1071.

The Normans, many of them second or third generation Christians, did not possess the cultural heritage which the English could trace back over a century and a half to King Alfred, and even earlier. They were, however, great builders and the most impressive surviving monuments of the age are the massive cathedrals and castle keeps, austere and majestic symbols of religious zeal and kingly authority. William I could neither read nor write, though he would hold a pen in his hand to put a crude autograph cross at the foot of charters issued in his name. Since there were virtually no educated laymen in northern Europe at this time, William and his successors were dependent upon church-men for their civil servants, their lawyers and their ad-ministrators. William was fortunate in securing the election of his friend Lanfranc as Archbishop of Canterbury in 1070. Lanfranc was an Italian by birth and a churchman learned in civil law as well as theology. His razor-sharp mind soon set in order the English Church, establishing a diocesan pattern which endured throughout the Middle Ages and encouraging the growth of ecclesiastical courts of law. But Lanfranc's greatest service to the monarchy was the encouragement of learning in monastic schools, thus ensuring a succession of 'clerks' who could hold government together even if a king's power was threatened

OPPOSITE A fanciful impression of Harold's death at William of Normandy's hands during the battle of Hastings. Whoever killed him, it was certainly not William.

16

Apres seynt Edward rey
na Harald le fiz Gode
wyn. count de kent. a forz
ea tort. ix. moys. dunke ve
ent Will bastard. e ly tol
yst la vye e le regne conquist
la tere. harald gist al walthm.

Puis regna Will bas
tard. xxi. an. puis mo
rust e gist a kame en
mundye.

King Stephen, from a contemporary manuscript.

Henry II quarrels with Becket.

HIC: WILLELM DVX: IVSSIT NAVES: EDIFICARE:

by private war among the barons. Improved efficiency in the eleventh-century Church guaranteed better government of the State. So long as it lasted, the partnership of sovereign and archbishop helped to civilize the militaristic character of Anglo-Norman feudalism.

Inevitably William spent much time in his later years protecting Normandy from the envious intrigues of his continental neighbours. He tended to look upon England as a source of revenue for his wars and he was forced to absent himself for long periods from the kingdom. Although he reigned for twenty-one years, he did not complete the settlement of the land he had won by his victory at Hastings. It was not until Christmas 1085 that he decided to send out commissioners to survey the whole of his realm. Within a year the two volumes known as the Domesday Book were ready for the King to study. But the survey was not complete, and it came too late for William to benefit from it. Early in 1087 war flared up again between William and King Philip I of France, and by the summer the Norman barons were campaigning in the Vexin, the disputed lands along the Seine between Rouen and Paris. In July William seized the town of Mantes and set fire to it. His horse reared up, he fell to the ground and received injuries from which he never recovered. On 9 September he died at Rouen and was buried at Caen.

ABOVE William, in council with Bishop Odo of Bayeux, gives orders for the building of an invasion fleet. Bayeux Tapestry.

BELOW Norman coinage – silver penny of William I.

ABOVE The seal of William I.

Less than three weeks after the Conqueror's death, his second surviving son was crowned by Lanfranc at Westminster, and the English lords paid homage to King William II. But many barons were faced by a difficult problem of loyalty. The duchy of Normandy passed into the hands of the Conqueror's eldest son, Robert (who had, at times, collaborated with Philip of France in campaigns against his own father). Many barons owned estates both in England and Normandy: whom should they serve? Some believed it would be simpler to oust William in Robert's favour, and there were rebellions in 1088 and 1095. But William was both a better soldier than Robert and a more quick-witted briber. Within four years he had isolated Robert politically and was virtually in control of Normandy himself. William and Robert between them combined to exclude their younger brother, Henry, from any territorial advantages. They distrusted his intellectual pretensions – for he could actually read – and they were envious of the considerable treasure in silver which their father had left to him.

The chroniclers had been in awe of William I. 'He was very dignified', one of them tells us, especially on the three occasions in the year when he sat crowned and enthroned before all the great men of England: 'at Easter in Winchester, at Whitsun in Westminster, at midwinter in Gloucester'. But there are no such passages of praise for his successor. William II offended the monastic chroniclers on four counts: his personal morals were lax; he treated the Church as a wealthy institution to be bled white by his tax-gatherers; he made Ranulf Flambard, the greediest of his financial advisers, Bishop of Durham; and, worst of all, he quarrelled with the saintly scholar, Anselm, whom he belatedly appointed Archbishop of Canterbury after having kept the see vacant for four years when Lanfranc died so that he could, as King, enjoy its revenues. Much of the money which William II and Flambard raised was squandered on a licentious court, where the King amused himself with strange practices. He was, we are told, short, fat, fair-haired, sharp-eyed and red-faced – hence his contemporary nickname, 'Rufus'. His principal recreation was hunting in the forest lands, which the Conqueror had placed under a particularly harsh protective law; and it seemed to contemporaries appropriate that Rufus should have been accidentally killed while hunting near Brockenhurst in the New Forest at the beginning of August 1100.

Yet Rufus's death was probably no accident. Henry – who, if Duke Robert were excluded, was next in line for the succession – was also hunting in the New Forest that day. Before nightfall he had ridden to Winchester and secured the royal treasury. Next morning he was proclaimed King and within three days he was at Westminster for coronation. Duke Robert was at this time in southern

OPPOSITE The bleak and forbidding keep of Richmond Castle, Yorkshire, a superb example of Norman military architecture.

LEFT Queen Matilda, from a History of England produced by the monks of St Albans.

OPPOSITE William II, known as William Rufus probably on account of his red hair.

Italy, returning from a crusade in which he much enhanced his reputation for soldierly chivalry. Rufus's death was opportune for Henry. A few weeks later Robert would have been home and able to challenge Henry's accession with a good prospect of success. As it was, Henry continued to court popularity speedily. A coronation charter promised 'the abolition of all the evil practices with which this realm of England was unjustly oppressed' in the previous reign. Ranulf Flambard was imprisoned in the Tower of London: Archbishop Anselm was recalled from exile. And fourteen weeks after his accession Henry married Matilda, the virtuous sister of the King of Scotland who had the additional merit of being a direct descendant

of Alfred the Great and the old Royal House of Wessex. With a new reign dawning so brightly for England, it is hardly surprising that favours subsequently bestowed by King Henry on the barons out hunting with Rufus that fateful August afternoon should have excited little comment. Henry I, who promised at his coronation to 'make the holy church of God free', could count on a good press from the chroniclers.

His reign did not fulfil these high expectations. Much of it was taken up with conflicts in Normandy and round the frontiers of the duchy. Robert unsuccessfully invaded England in 1101 and, though a compromise settlement was reached, the rift between the two brothers became so great

Oꝛa caiuiꞇ geſta Ꝛuſium ꝓꝛaꝺo foꝛeſta
Ꞷillm ꝛapiuiꞇ moꝛꞅꝛ ſagiꞇta fuiꞇ

that, on the fortieth anniversary of Hastings, their armies fought a decisive encounter at Tinchebrai, a castle thirty miles inland from Avranches. The English invaders overwhelmed the forces of ducal Normandy, and Robert – who lived to be eighty – was imprisoned by his brother for the remaining twenty-eight years of his life at Wareham, Devizes, Bristol and finally Cardiff. But the Norman campaigns continued, despite Duke Robert's incarceration, and they absorbed more and more of Henry's revenue.

Soon, Henry's relations with the Church became little happier than those of Rufus had been. Although he avoided an open quarrel with Anselm, the Archbishop was incensed by his insistence on appointing abbots and bishops and investing them with their sacred symbols of office. 'Lay investiture' of this kind was roundly condemned by the popes, who denied the right of kings to carry out any religious ceremonies, since they were not priests but laymen. Reluctantly Henry recognized that the Church was reducing kingship to the level of a purely secular profession. He bound the higher clergy to render homage to him as great landowners. At the same time, he became far less a champion of 'God's free and holy church'. After Anselm's death in 1109 he exploited the wealth of Canterbury for twelve months longer than even Rufus had done when Lanfranc died. In 1128–9 Henry personally was enjoying the revenues from the bishoprics of both Coventry and

Durham, which he deliberately left vacant for several years. Angry protests arrived with ominous regularity from Rome. He ignored them.

Unlike Rufus, Henry never scoffed cynically at religion nor shocked contemporaries by outbursts of blasphemy. No one could describe him as virtuous, for he was the father of at least twenty children born out of wedlock. It is said that in the first instance he advanced the career of his later justiciar, Roger of Salisbury, because he sang the Latin mass faster than any other priest at Henry's court; but at least the King regularly heard mass. He was, it appears, deeply moved when his courtier Rahere told him how he had vowed to found a hospital if he recovered from malarial fever contracted on a pilgrimage to Rome. Rahere gained from Henry a site for an Augustinian priory at Smithfield; and London gained from Rahere the first of its hospitals, dedicated to St Bartholomew. In later years the Londoners looked back in gratitude to Henry I for his patronage of Rahere, and the chroniclers welcomed his encouragement of the new, reformed monasticism of the Cluniacs.

Henry achieved much for England. He saw the need to establish a civil service and a centralized exchequer in order to hold government together. Under his rule there were no serious rebellions in the kingdom for a third of a century. The law was often a harsh instrument but it was reasonably uniform and just; and the barons were kept in their place. But disaster threatened throughout Henry's last years. In November 1120 his only legitimate son, William, was drowned when the most up-to-date vessel in the Channel, the *White Ship*, struck a rock off Barfleur. Who now would claim the throne on Henry's death? Matilda, his only daughter, was married to the Emperor Henry V and had not lived in England since she was a child of eight. The most likely claimant was Duke Robert's son, William Clito, an enemy of almost all the English baronage. But Robert himself was still alive, and many barons supported Stephen of Blois, a son of the Conqueror's youngest daughter. Stephen was Henry I's favourite nephew.

Henry lived for fifteen years after the wreck of the *White Ship* but the succession question continued to plague him. Death removed William Clito in a skirmish, Duke Robert, and the Emperor Henry V. In June 1128 Matilda, at twenty-five, took as a second husband Geoffrey of Anjou, the fourteen-year-old heir to a rich duchy. A son — the future Henry II — was born at Le Mans in March 1133 and King Henry travelled across to Rouen hoping to settle the succession problem for all time. Unfortunately he found Matilda detested by his nobles and supremely tactless in manner. Stephen's prospects improved rapidly. When the King died on 1 December 1133 – having ruined his digestion with a dish of lampreys, forbidden by his

doctor – Stephen seized the initiative. He hurried across the Channel and was welcomed by the people of London. Within four weeks he was crowned at Westminster and within six he had received recognition from Pope Innocent II. Technically Stephen was King of England for the remaining nineteen years of his life.

For most of Stephen's reign England was rent by civil war. The collapse of centralized power played into the hands of the barons and principal ecclesiastics. Stephen was a prisoner for several years and it seemed likely that Matilda would be crowned, despite her unpopularity in London. But there was no settled political pattern. Matilda herself came near to capture in Oxford Castle which Stephen besieged for the last quarter of the year 1142. Henry of Huntingdon describes how Matilda 'escaped across the frozen Thames, dressed in white cloaks, tricking the besiegers' eyes in the dazzle of the snow'. But these years of anarchy possess few such picturesque scenes. The barons were no better than feudal gangsters, changing allegiance at the drop of a charter of privileges and demanding protection money to spare the countryside or save an abbey from plunder. 'They said openly that Christ and his saints were asleep', a chronicler recalled a few years later. Never had the yoke of the Anglo-Norman system borne down so heavily on the King's wretched subjects.

At last, in November 1153, a compromise settlement was reached at Winchester between the rival power groups. Stephen would reign unmolested for his lifetime and adopt Matilda's son, Henry Plantagenet, as his heir. Eleven months later Stephen died at Dover Castle. A young man of twenty-one inherited an almost powerless throne.

ABOVE Silver penny of Henry I's reign, showing him crowned and holding a sceptre.

OPPOSITE Four early medieval kings: (left to right, from the top) William I, William Rufus, Henry I and Stephen.

2
Power of the Throne
1164~1272

ENRY PLANTAGENET, Count of Anjou, was ruler of vast continental territories even before he was crowned King of England on 19 December 1154. He gained Normandy from his mother and became lord of Anjou, Maine and Touraine on his father's death in September 1151. Eight months later, still only nineteen, he startled feudal Europe by marrying Eleanor of Aquitaine. She was a dark beauty eleven years his senior, with a devastating intelligence and a love life so scandalous that one admiring monk wrote, with spicy discretion, 'Hush! Let nothing more be said of it, though I know it well.' Eleanor had already been married for fourteen years to the King of France but, since she failed to provide him with a son, their union was annulled. She had greater success with Henry – five boys and three girls in fifteen years. But her chief value in Henry's eyes was her possessions, lands reaching down the Biscayan coast to Bayonne and inland to the hills of Auvergne. When, soon after his accession, Henry II absorbed Brittany he became master of an empire which stretched for 750 miles from the Cheviots in the north to the Pyrenees in the south, a territorial bloc broken only by the Channel. It was the largest composite empire in western Europe, even though it lacked any natural cohesion.

These French possessions dictated Henry II's policy. He lived for more than half his reign outside England, and it was therefore essential for him to establish in England a judicial and administrative system which would ensure obedience to government even in the absence of the sovereign. In creating a system of royal courts with the King's Justices travelling throughout the land, Henry was not consciously endowing his kingdom with a code of Common Law. He was applying a practical solution to the problem of asserting royal justice and restraining the arbitrary decisions of baronial misrule. The growth of a jury system – the most remarkable consequence of Henry's legal reforms – was largely accidental; and it seemed to him of less importance than the Assize regulations forbidding the fortifying of castles without royal

licence and decreeing what weapons and armour were to be borne by the various ranks of his subjects. Many of Henry II's administrative measures were far from popular, for itinerant Justices were responsible for collecting revenue as well as maintaining the King's peace. But there was a businesslike quality in the form of the new chancery writs, a sign of continuity in administration and a reflection of the King's legalistic insistence on points of detail.

It is hard to see in Henry II the great-grandson of the Conqueror. Physically, perhaps, there is some resemblance: the same stocky frame, prematurely corpulent. But Henry was a scholar, well educated and naturally intelligent. He is the first English King of whom it was said that he retired to his chamber with a book after the day's business was completed. Not that he was an intellectual. He liked hunting, hawking and womanizing. Rosamund Clifford ('fair Rosamund'), his mistress at Woodstock in 1174–5, became a revered figure in folk legend and when she died in 1176 he made her tomb at Godstow as ornate as the shrine of a saint. But there are other more nebulous figures. Who was the 'Bellebelle' who shares with Queen Eleanor an entry for the purchase of gowns in the exchequer accounts of 1184?

Although Henry liked to hold court at forested lodges in good hunting country – at Clarendon in Wiltshire and at Woodstock in Oxfordshire, for example – he was a diligent worker. His energy and contempt for regular routine hours exhausted his secretaries. 'I hardly dare say it', one of them wrote in a letter, 'but I honestly believe he delights in putting us into a fix.' He selected his officials personally, irrespective of their social standing, and he would remove them ruthlessly at any sign of incompetence or neglect. His treasurers, chancellors and justiciars were all men of high quality.

Yet Henry was remembered throughout the Middle Ages for one disastrous appointment. In 1162 he persuaded his friend Thomas Becket (Chancellor for the past seven years) to be consecrated Archbishop of Canterbury. Henry hoped Becket would help him bring the ecclesiastical

The assassination of Thomas
à Becket, from a French
illuminated book of hours.

Apres henry le secund regna Richard sun fiz. x. aunze
demy sil entre payzand de la tere seynt fust pris del duk
de Osterit par eyde del roy phylippe de fraunce. e fust reynt hors
de prison pur cent mil lyueres de argent. e pur cel tauncun su
erent les Chaliz de Engletere pris. des Eglyses e venduz. Puis
fust tret de vn quarel de Alblast al chastel de chalezun. dist
cete vers sit fet: Xpe tui calicis: predo sit preda calicis.

LEFT Two scenes from the life of Richard I. On the left he is seen imprisoned in Germany, and on the right he is mortally wounded by crossbowmen at Chalus.

RIGHT Richard I's coronation. The strong English presence in France is symbolized by the burning fortress of Gisors, the key to the defences of Normandy.

courts into line with the royal courts but the Archbishop felt bound to defend church privileges, even though many of them were abuses of recent origin. Becket, in a long quarrel, seemed more than once to be inconsistent, while Henry tried with reckless speed to define the precise rights of the Church, limiting its authority over criminal matters as he had limited the opportunities of the barons to wage private war. Becket escaped into exile in 1164, was reconciled with the King six years later, but on his return to England seemed as intransigent as ever. Henry, in Normandy, was enraged to hear of Becket's obstinacy and complained that this low-born clerk was mocking his sovereign lord. Four knights of the King's household were so impressed by this extraordinary scene of royal anger that they crossed to England and assassinated Becket in Canterbury Cathedral on 29 December 1170.

Henry was appalled by the news of the Archbishop's murder. Soon Becket, by no means popular in his lifetime, became a cult figure. He was canonized within twenty-six months of his martyrdom and Henry accepted the humiliation of a public penance although he declared on oath he had never sought the Archbishop's death. Politically Henry suffered little from the knights' rash action: the problem of the ecclesiastical courts was settled by a compromise with papal representatives in 1172, largely by judiciously ignoring questions which had seemed of high principle to the martyred Becket. Nevertheless the whole dramatic episode – on which there is more contemporary written material than on any other single event in the Middle Ages – confirmed widespread tales of Henry's uncontrollable rages. All the Angevin rulers, it was said, were descended from Satan's daughter. 'From the Devil he came', complained St Bernard of Clairvaux when Henry was young, 'and to the Devil he shall return.' Many of the King's subjects, tormented by their sovereign's fickle passions of wrath, would have agreed with him.

The Angevin empire was too cumbersome for any ruler unless he were by nature an able diplomat and soldier.

LEFT King John out stag-hunting, from a fourteenth-century manuscript.

OPPOSITE John was never a popular king – this manuscript illustration shows him being offered a cup of poisoned wine.

Henry, conscious of this burden, planned to partition his lands between his sons so as to ensure a smooth succession. They were however an ungrateful, suspicious and envious brood, quarrelling among themselves and ready to rebel against their father. They hoped to compel him to hand over sovereign powers to them even in his own lifetime. Their greed was exploited by Henry's enemies in France, and at times they were encouraged by their mother, Eleanor, who was estranged from the King for the last twenty years of his life. She doted on her fourth son, Richard. Henry however preferred John, the youngest of the family, whom he nicknamed 'Lackland' because, as a child, it was not easy to find a portion of the Angevin bounty for him to inherit. When, in the summer of 1189, Henry learnt that John, too, had rebelled against him, the bitter blow completed his disillusionment. He died in his castle at Chinon two days after learning of John's treachery and he was buried twelve miles away at Fontevrault Abbey, in death as in life an Angevin rather than an Englishman.

Henry's elaborate plans for dividing his empire were superfluous. Three sons died before him and the whole Angevin succession passed to his fourth child, Richard. More than two years before Henry's death, Richard had pledged himself to set out for the Holy Land on the Third Crusade, an enterprise of western Christendom to free Jerusalem from the Moslem ruler Saladin. Family disputes delayed his departure but he was determined to go as soon

as he could leave his inheritance in reasonable order'. He crossed to England on 13 August 1189, was crowned three weeks later at Westminster and returned to Normandy a fortnight before Christmas, having entrusted the administration to one of his principal advisers in Aquitaine, William Longchamp. Richard did not set foot in the kingdom again until March 1194, when he stayed for two months. The remainder of his days he spent in France. He was therefore resident in England for only twenty-five weeks during his ten-year reign.

Richard I, 'the Lion Heart', won wide renown for his soldierly qualities. He conquered Cyprus (which was in Greek rather than Moslem hands), recovered the city of Acre, advanced to within a dozen miles of Jerusalem, and won an outstanding victory against the Moslem Saracens at Jaffa. Unfortunately he also quarrelled bitterly with his fellow Christian Princes, who were far from sharing his mother Eleanor's opinion that among them Richard stood out as 'the great one and the good'. On his return from Acre, his ship was wrecked in the Adriatic (December 1192) and Richard was kept in prison in Austria by the Emperor Henry VI who maintained that he had insulted his son during the fighting at Acre. The English and Norman people had to pay a ransom of £100,000 for the release of their absentee king. The money was speedily raised, thanks to the efficiency of the administrative system left by Henry II, but during his imprisonment Richard's

Continued on pg 34

pres richard regna son sun frere en ky tens Englete
fuist entredyt. vi. aunz e. iii. quarters e. i. moys par
la pape. Innocent pur mestre Esteuen de langeton. ke le roy
ne vout receyuere a Ercoueke de kaunterbyrs. Sistoyt
dunk le grant guere entre ly e les barons noirays Dunt vent
sir Lowys fiz le roy Phylippe de fraunce en Engletere : le
roy son regna. xvii. aunz e demy. puis vent a Swynesheued
e fuist enpoysone par une frere de la meson si come tu dit
e le roy morust a Neulwerk e sun cors fuist entere a Wyrcet

LEFT Crusade fever gripped Europe in the twelfth century. This peasants' crusade is from a French manuscript entitled *Livres des Passages d'Outremer*.

RIGHT The religious justification – the returning crusader receives absolution from a priest.

ABOVE Crusaders bombarding Nicosia with the decapitated heads of their prisoners.

LEFT A knight removing his mail shirt, from an Arabic manuscript.

RIGHT A crusader paying homage.

THE CRUSADES

In November 1095 Pope Urban II summoned a council at Clermont in France and exhorted the Christian princes of Europe to take up arms in a holy war. In the east the growing might of Islam threatened the holy city of Jerusalem and the once-great empire of Byzantium was no longer able to defend the heart of medieval Christianity.

Newly invigorated by Gregorian reforms, Western Christianity responded enthusiastically to the challenge. Jerusalem, the earthly symbol of the heavenly city, had long been an important centre of pilgrimage despite the hazardous nature of the journey. Now the tradition of pilgrimage – not only as an act of devotion but also of penance – was given new emphasis by the Crusades. Moreover the war against the infidel was regarded as a religious undertaking and Urban granted plenary indulgences (the remission of all penance for sin) to all who 'took the cross'. Stressing the plight to Eastern Christians, the danger to pilgrims and the desecration of holy places, the Pope urged men to turn their energies to a holy cause.

On the political front, European leaders recognized the threat that the Seljuks could pose to their own lands if allowed to advance unchecked. In addition they welcomed the opportunity to divert their restless and turbulent subjects from domestic quarrels. But the crusades not only satisfied the dictates of piety and politics. With the feudal structure of society and its code of chivalry, Europe was undoubtedly well equipped militarily to meet the challenge of such an enterprise. Here the craving for battle and chivalry was neatly combined with the prospect of adventure and plunder.

The First Crusade set out in 1096, its forces swelled by a rabble of landless peasants, thieves and beggars. Benefiting from the temporary disarray of the Seljuk army, the crusaders took the city of Antioch after a siege of nine months. Then in July 1099 they entered Jerusalem. The Moslem inhabitants of the city were slaughtered, and Godfrey de Boullion was elected Defender of the Holy Sepulchre. Four Latin states were set up, fortified with magnificent castles. Two military orders, the Knights Templar and the Order of St John, were established to protect the pilgrim route to the city. Later they assumed much of the burden of defending the crusader states.

In 1187 the brilliant Saracen leader Saladin wiped out the crusader forces at the Horns of Hittin and recaptured Jerusalem. In response a new expedition, the Third Crusade, was launched, led by Philip Augustus of France and Richard 1 of England. (The Second Crusade, an abortive attempt headed by Louis VII of France, had ended in dismal failure.) Richard the Lion Heart epitomized the crusader legend of knights in shining armour riding out against the infidel. In fact, of the eight major crusades, the third was probably the most bloody and brutal affair. After taking Cyprus, Richard besieged Acre. When the city surrendered the inhabitants were massacred. Richard failed to reach Jerusalem and was forced to make a treaty with Saladin.

The later crusades were largely disastrous. The leaders of the Fourth Crusade, diverted from their religious mission by the prospect of plunder, sacked Constantinople and all but destroyed Europe's most effective bastion in the east. As a result the Turks rapidly advanced westward and by the fifteenth century threatened to strike at the heart of Europe. Gradually the rising cost of such expeditions, the decline of that vital sense of common purpose, ecclesiastical and political differences and the changing nature of feudalism brought an end to the era of the crusades. In 1291 Acre, the last crusader stronghold on the mainland, fell to the Turks.

ABOVE The personal seal of Robert Fitzwalter, an English crusader.

RIGHT Krak des Chevaliers, a crusader castle in Syria.

possessions in Normandy and Touraine were threatened by the King of France, and the whole Angevin empire seemed to be tottering to the ground.

While Richard was on crusade and in prison, his brother John had followed a devious and treacherous policy of intrigue. He had encouraged opposition to William Longchamp and other barons given posts of responsibility by the King. Shortly before Richard embarked for home, John travelled to Paris and agreed to render homage to King Philip of France for the Angevin lands. He then crossed back to England and began to stir up rebellion. These schemes were frustrated by the energetic action of the Queen Mother (then in her seventieth year) and by the royal justiciars. Once Richard was liberated he pardoned John, who behaved loyally for the remaining five years of the reign. The King himself concentrated on checking French incursions into his ancestral possessions. The new fortress of Château Gaillard – a brilliant achievement of military engineering – dominated the Seine valley at Les Andelys and effectively defended Normandy. But Richard could not complete his work and secure a lasting peace in France. At the end of March 1199 he was wounded, while not wearing armour, in a trivial skirmish. Gangrene set in and he died soon afterwards. He designated John to succeed him in England and Normandy, but the barons of Anjou

ABOVE A page of Magna Carta – an ordinary-looking document, but one with far-reaching consequences for England (though it had little immediate effect). The Charter's sixty-one clauses reflected closely the mood of the times: foreign mercenaries to be expelled; Welsh hostages to be released; merchants to have free passage in peacetime; and, most significant of all, curbs on the King's arbitrary authority – 'To none shall we sell, or deny, or delay right of justice'.

OPPOSITE The crusaders were Christians in the narrowest sense – Richard I watches the systematic beheading of the entire Moslem garrison at Acre in 1191.

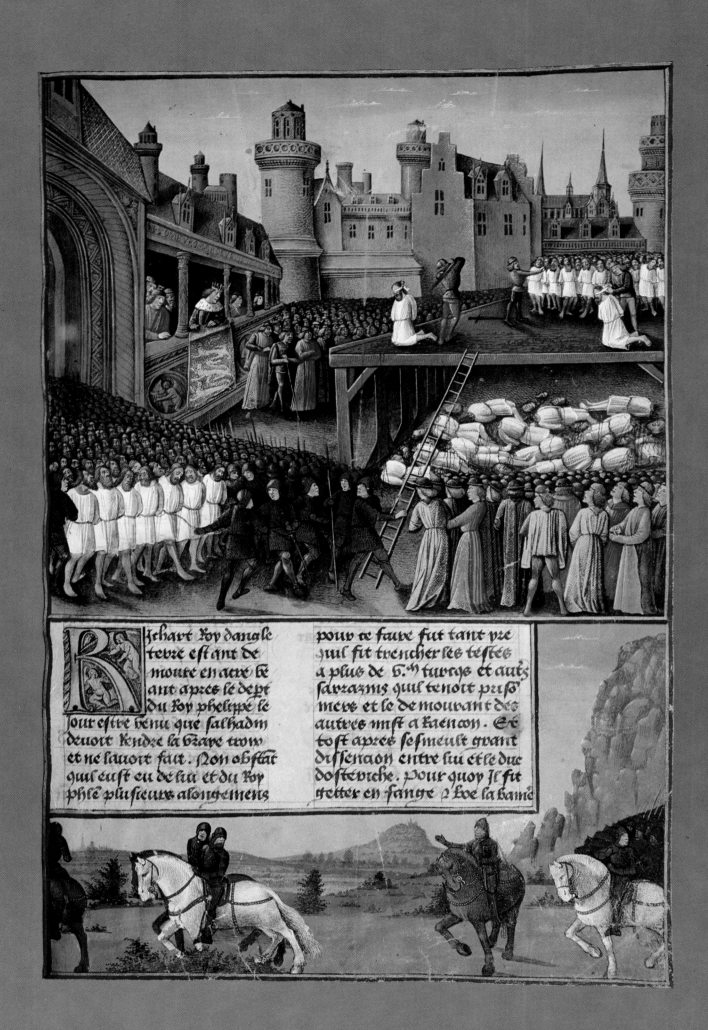

Richart Roy dangle
terre estant de
moute en mer se
ant apres le dept
du Roy phelippe se
iour estre venu que salhadin
deuoit rendre la vraye crow
et ne sauoit fait. Non obstat
quil eust eu de sui et du Roy
phle plusieurs alongemens

pour ce faire fut tant yre
quil fit trencher les testes
a plus de b.M turcks et autz
sarrazins quil tenoit priso
mere et le demourant des
autres mist a rancon. Et
tost apres se smeult grant
dissenacio entre sui et le duc
dosterriche. Pour quoy Il fit
ietter en sanse s boe la banie

longtam voyage : quil souffra de porter seulemet vng
lac de soye a vng ymage de samct george pendat a icellui.
Aussi se sedit colier dor auoit besoing de reparacion il pora
estre mise en la main de louurier iusques a ce quil soit
repare. Lequel colier aussi ne pourra estre enrichy de
pierres ou daultres choses reserue ses ymage qui pourra
estre garny au plaisir du cheualier. Et aussi ne pourra
estre sedit colier vendu engaige donne ne aliene pour
necessite ou cause quelconque que ce soit

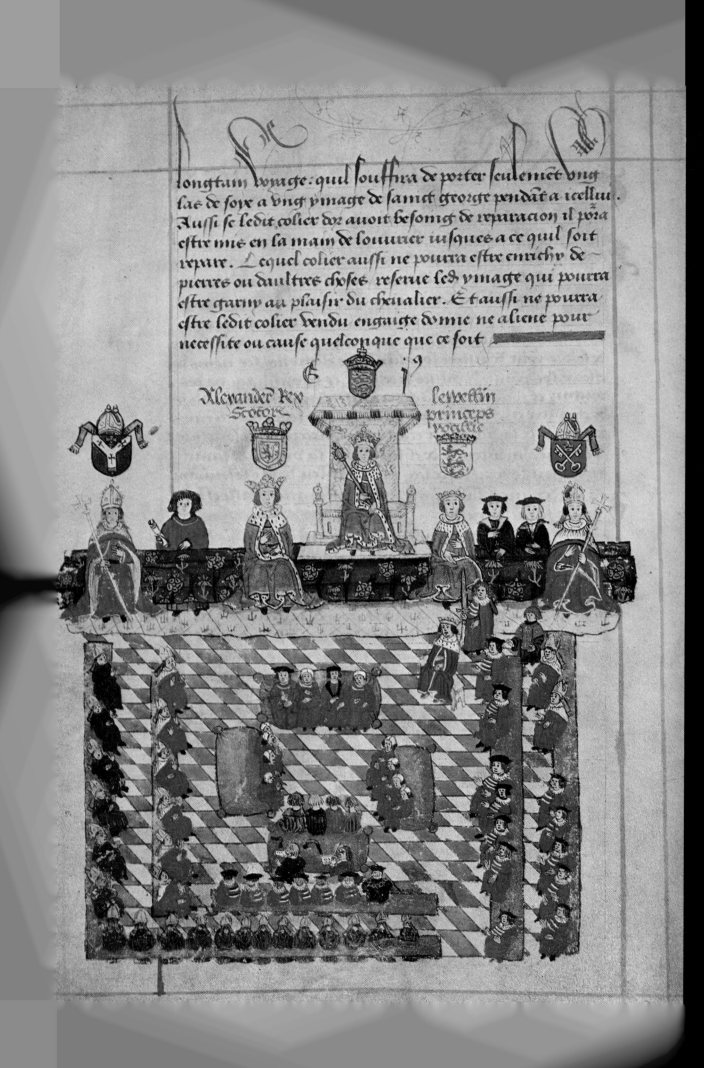

Alexander Rex
Scotois

lewellin
princeps
wallie

swore allegiance to the twelve-year-old Arthur of Brittany (a nephew of Richard and John).

A monk of St Albans declared after John's death, 'Now the filth of Hell is made fouler still by his presence.' And for six centuries the historians were no more generous than the chroniclers to the King's reputation. In recent years it has become clear he was a good strategist, an energetic worker and an able administrator. He was personally fastidious, taking baths regularly twice a month, and he is the first English king of whom it is recorded that he possessed a dressing gown. The monks of Beaulieu Abbey (which he founded) and the cathedrals of Chichester and Worcester (where he is buried) honoured his memory, whatever the monks of St Albans might think. But it is difficult to rehabilitate him convincingly. Like Richard I, he may have sought unity, stability and peace in France, but he failed dismally. Moreover there is little doubt that he personally killed his nephew Arthur in a drunken rage at Rouen in April 1203, having captured him after a creditable exercise in military initiative the previous August. It was John's reputation for arbitrary acts of cruelty which made the baronage unwilling to support him in Normandy. In the first week of December 1203 he abandoned defence of the duchy, leaving the barons to make their own terms with Philip of France.

Yet, from 1205 onwards, John devoted his energy to preparing expeditions which would recover his position in France. Extraordinarily heavy taxation was imposed upon the English at a time when prices were rising generally and the medieval economy experiencing the unwelcome novelty of inflation. John's military expenditure made him unpopular but he was also foolish enough to incur hostility from the Church by contesting with the papacy the election of an Archbishop of Canterbury. Innocent III, the most forceful of all popes, wanted the scholarly Stephen Langton as archbishop, and John did not. To impose his will Innocent placed England under an interdict in 1208: all religious observances were suspended, including services of baptism, marriage and burial. When John, in return, seized church revenues he was duly excommunicated by the Pope.

It says much for the power of the throne that John could survive several years of interdict during which he was stretching the laws so as to raise heavier and heavier taxes. Yet not until the closing months of 1212 was he faced with a serious threat of rebellion. The danger, however, induced him the following spring to make peace with the Pope. He accepted Langton as archbishop, and, in a characteristically feudal act, resigned his kingdom to Innocent III, receiving

it back in return for an annual monetary tribute, paid by successive English rulers (somewhat irregularly) to the popes for the next century and a half. Pope Innocent thereby became John's protector and ally in his struggles against the French and his rebellious baronage.

John staked everything on victory in the war with Philip of France. Initially all went well. A French invasion fleet was destroyed in combined operations by sea and landing parties against Damme, the port of Bruges, in May 1213. John's strategic instincts were sound: a northern attack on France by his allies in Flanders, a southern assault on Anjou from a base at La Rochelle. But the pincer movement failed to pinch. John's southern enterprise was ruined by massive desertions among the baronage, and his allies were overwhelmingly defeated in the decisive battle of Bouvines on 27 July 1214. John, isolated at La Rochelle, abandoned any attempt to recover his lost lands and returned to England.

There the baronage, furious at the extortionate taxes of the past eight years, were already in arms against their lord. Archbishop Langton sought to mediate, converting a feudal rebellion into a movement for reforms which would check the arbitrary abuse of law and custom by the King. Langton's moderation was reflected in the terms of the Great Charter, a comprehensive definition of feudal liberties and obligations to which John authorized attachment of his seal at Runnymede, between Staines and Windsor, in June 1215. But neither the extreme insurgents among the baronage nor the King himself were satisfied by the terms of Magna Carta. Civil war continued for two more years after Runnymede, with the barons seeking and receiving considerable aid from France. When in October 1216 John died suddenly from dysentery at Newark he left his nine-year-old son Henry a kingdom in which London and half the counties were in the hands of rebellious barons and their French partners.

Fortunately for Henry III he was served by two able Regents, William Marshal and Hubert de Burgh, who defeated the foreign interventionists and broke the insurgent barons. It was not until January 1227 that Henry assumed full sovereignty over the kingdom. He was intelligent, devout and sensitive to beauty, a great patron of Gothic art with the rebuilt abbey church of Westminster his lasting memorial. Chroniclers often mention his simplicity of spirit and praise the happiness and virtue of his family life. He married Eleanor of Provence in 1236, and their hospitality attracted to England not merely her relatives, but other well-born foreigners ambitious for advancement. French aristocratic immigrants won for themselves the top appointments in both Church and State, arousing a vigorous nationalistic backlash among the English baronage and among the townsfolk of London and

OPPOSITE Edward I presides over his Parliament.

other boroughs. By 1258 the new baronial opposition, seeking reform of government, had found a leader in Simon de Montfort, Earl of Leicester, who married Henry III's youngest sister in 1238.

Basically Earl Simon and the barons wanted royal policy controlled by a council, half chosen by themselves and half by the sovereign, and advised by an assembly – the 'Parliamentum' – which should meet three times a year. Between 1258 and 1264 Henry vacillated, sometimes supporting Earl Simon, sometimes seeking to promote quarrels in the baronial opposition. In the spring of 1264 the tension between the opposing sides led to a civil war. Earl Simon defeated the King and his eldest son Edward at Lewes and, for a year, sought a settlement which would have provided for a Parliament (with representatives from the larger towns). But Earl Simon had too many adversaries among the baronage, whose discontent was exploited by the heir to the throne. In May 1265 Edward escaped from surveillance and rallied royalist support to free Henry III from the restraints allegedly imposed upon him since the battle of Lewes. There was little hope for Simon de Montfort. He was cornered at Evesham on 4 August and perished in battle. The King himself was a helpless spectator, hemmed in by Earl Simon's knights as Edward's royalists hacked their way to Henry's rescue. At twenty-six the future Edward I had shown himself a soldier of courage and initiative and a staunch upholder of kingly power. But it was the dead Earl, with his unrealized plans of reform, who became the legendary hero among the people.

Henry died in November 1272 and though Edward was on crusade and in Sicily, no challenge was offered to his succession.

ABOVE In 1257 Henry III introduced the first gold penny since the Norman Conquest, but it failed to find favour and was eventually withdrawn.

OPPOSITE The effigy of Henry III, from Westminster Abbey.

3
Three Edwards
1272~1377

DWARD I was thirty-three years old at his accession. He was unusually tall and slim – hence his nickname 'Longshanks'–and until early middle age he retained the figure of an athlete. Along with this striking physique there went a clear and decisive manner of speech, and a willingness to seek advice and to benefit from it. No English sovereign since the Conqueror had ascended the throne with such a wealth of military and administrative experience behind him. Though he may have inherited drooping eyelids from his father, there was little of Henry III in his character. He combined the crusader ideal of his great-uncle, Richard I, with the tidy, legalistic mind of his great-grandfather, Henry II. Even before his accession, he was respected as a warrior in western Europe and the Middle East. He hoped, once he had settled the affairs of his realm, to lead a grand crusade which would finally liberate Jerusalem from the Moslem Saracens. As he grew older he came to realize, with increasing bitterness, that the problems of England were too vast for him to serve militant Christendom in Syria and Palestine, but he never entirely abandoned his dream of fulfilling Richard I's purpose. As late as the year 1300, in the middle of a campaign against the Scots, Edward sought to justify his military activity to the Archbishop of Canterbury by citing the sixty-second chapter of Isaiah, 'For Zion's sake will I not hold my peace, and for Jerusalem's sake I will not rest, until the righteousness thereof go forth as brightness.' Edward's spiritual vision extended to a far more distant horizon than the Welsh mountains and Scottish lowlands which enshrine his military reputation.

No one, however, would remember him as a religious fanatic. He was, above all, a law-maker and a just interpreter of rights and customs. The weakness of the central government during the long reign of Henry III had allowed many abuses to creep into the administration. Barons claimed a local jurisdiction for which, all too often, there was scant justification: Edward's legal reforms made sure that feudal obligations were honoured; a landowner was required to explain by what right (*Quo Warranto*) he held his land and

ABOVE No doubt swallowing his scruples, Edward I pays homage to the French king. His son Edward II married a princess of France.

OPPOSITE An artist's imaginative impression of Edward I returning to London from a crusade, an ambition he never in fact achieved.

A Londres vint p sojourner
M joec su tot le pner

J loec par maledie languist
C t mozut amy dien wnfist
J loec estert enseuelee
a Westmouster p solempure
E dwarð sun fiz apres regnast
Cil tuit la terre si le gardast
Cil fu de grant prestise
E il meintint bien ses franchises
De seint Eglie a mult samott
K entres a possessiuns saun seurs

ABOVE Edward I returns by ship from Gascony, an English possession at this time.

OPPOSITE Grief-stricken at the death of Queen Eleanor, Edward I ordered crosses to be erected at every halt her funeral procession made on its return to London. This is the Northampton Cross.

exercised the powers of jurisdiction which he claimed. Henceforth all rights had to be clearly defined and checks were imposed on the transfer of land and obligations both by the barons and by the churchmen. These reforms were of lasting significance. They provided England with a framework of Statute Law, the essential basis of a flexible and unwritten constitution. At the same time Edward emphasized the importance of continuity in the administration of justice by encouraging the growth of the existing courts of law and by instituting the first word by word reports of legal proceedings, a lasting repository of Common Law tradition.

Legalistic reform was not the only constitutional development of the reign. Edward followed the precedent of Simon de Montfort in summoning national assemblies which became known as Parliaments. But, while Montfort's initiative was essentially revolutionary, Edward I sought a permanent institution where the sovereign could make contact with representatives of the differing layers of society. No doubt the prime virtue of a parliament, in Edward's eyes, was that it simplified the assessment and levying of taxes but the records of these assemblies show that they also discussed general questions of government, including foreign affairs. By the end of the thirteenth century knights and burgesses were regularly attending the King or his Chancellor in the 'High Court of Parliament', although their presence was consultative rather than legislative in character. It was never intended that the community should impose its will upon the King's Majesty.

Institutional development reflects a ruler's capacity for good government: it does not, however, capture his personality. Unlike many contemporary warrior kings, Edward lived a happy family life. At the age of fifteen he married Eleanor of Castile. Their union was a strategic device to protect the Plantagenet possessions in Gascony, but it became a love match. They had sixteen children, nine of whom died young. Eleanor herself contracted a fever in the autumn of 1290 and died at Harby in Nottinghamshire. The desolate Edward ordered crosses to be erected at the nine places where Eleanor's coffin rested on its journey south to Westminster. Three of these crosses survive: at Geddington, Hardingstone and Waltham. A few months later Edward commissioned a gilded bronze effigy of his dead Queen to be cast for her marble shrine in Westminster Abbey. Together the Eleanor Crosses and the elaborate tomb emphasize a tender humanity in Edward's character which is necessarily lacking in the statutes and

Continued on pg 47

ABOVE Symbolic print of death coming to claim its victims – rich and poor, young and old – from a printer's workshop.

BELOW The Black Death swept through Europe, leaving no country untouched, before it reached England. This is a German *Pestblatt* carried to protect the owner from pestilence.

ABOVE Card carried as a lucky charm to ward off the plague.

BELOW Even the presence of three doctors at the bedside of a rich victim cannot save him.

The summer of 1348 was fine and warm, with every prospect of a good harvest. Suddenly, in August, disaster struck a number of villages in south Dorset. A mysterious contagious illness spread rapidly from home to home. When news of the disease reached first Winchester and later London it was recognized as similar to the plague which had swept in the previous two years through trading communities along the Danube and the Rhine. That spring it had appeared in Brittany, and it was presumably carried to the Dorset harbours by vessels plying regularly across the Channel. Nobody knew its origins, nor indeed how it spread and how to combat it. Modern opinion believes there were two forms of plague, both originating in Asia: one was pneumonic and spread by contact; the other was bubonic and spread by rats from one filthy township to another. By the autumn it had leapt from Dorset through Somerset to Exeter in the west and to Bristol in the north, where it killed more than a third of the inhabitants. By November 1348 it was in London, by January 1349 in Norwich, and then it spread northwards up the east coast and even into Scotland. Nothing so terrible had been known before within the British Isles: men called this visitation 'the Black Death'.

It is impossible to tell how many people died in 1348–9. There was no proper record of the living population, let alone of deaths. Estimates can only be made from detailed studies of particular districts. Some villages were wiped out entirely; in others the surviving population fled to what it hoped was a healthier site. From the records of changes in the parish clergy it seems as if nearly half of the local priests in the dioceses of Ely, Exeter, Lincoln, Norwich, Winchester and York succumbed. Over the country as a whole in 1348–50 about one person in five appears to have died from the plague, with a higher mortality among adults than children. The Black Death returned in 1361–2 (when it carried away more youngsters than before) and again in 1369. The cumulative effect of all these visitations led, by the end of the century, to a reduction of the population by a third, possibly even by half.

Similar epidemics continued to devastate English cities intermittently for the next three centuries. They reached a climax with the Plague of London of 1665. Thereafter the bubonic plague disappeared from the British Isles, probably because brown rats killed off the medieval plague-flea-carrying black rats.

The Black Death had more significant social and economic consequences than the other visitations. Already landowners had begun to rely on paid peasant labour rather than on the bonded serf of earlier feudalism. As a result of the Black Death the market value of a peasant labourer doubled; and unfree villeins began to seek the right to take their labour where it would be best rewarded. The later fourteenth century saw the first serious stirrings of social unrest in the countryside.

ABOVE St Roch, the patron saint of plague sufferers.

RIGHT Tusmore, Oxfordshire, Marks in the fields show the position of a village deserted at the time of the Black Death and never reoccupied.

parliamentary writs that constitute the principal memorial of his reign.

It is lacking, too, in the most impressive of Edward I's monuments, the thick walls and drum-towers of his Welsh castles – Flint, Rhuddlan, Conway, Caernarvon, Beaumaris, Denbigh, Criccieth and Harlech. Earlier Anglo-Norman armies had passed through the Welsh valleys; the so-called 'Marcher Lords' had established a hold on southern Wales and fortified Cardigan, Carmarthen and Aberystwyth; but it was Edward who first sought to subjugate the hardy mountaineers of Snowdonia. The Welsh Prince, Llywelyn ap Gruffydd, had used the baronial disputes of Henry III's reign as an opportunity to increase his power at the expense of the Marcher Lords and to encourage his people to think, once more, of a Wales independent of England. Llywelyn's statecraft provoked Edward into fighting a vigorous campaign during the summer of 1277, advancing along the coast of North Wales so as to cut off the Welsh from their supplies in Anglesey. Five years later the Welsh were in arms again, and Edward raised a large army from England and from Gascony in order to control them. Llywelyn was killed and Edward imposed a 'Statute of Wales' on the principality, seeking to assimilate its customs and peoples to the English system of administration. In this policy Edward was not entirely successful. Welsh national pride continued to erupt from time to time in revolt. In 1301 Edward sought to reconcile the Welsh to the Plantagenet dynasty by having his eldest surviving son, the sixteen-year-old Edward of Caernarvon, proclaimed Prince of Wales at a solemn ceremony at Lincoln. But it needed more than empty pageantry to reconcile the Welsh to alien authority. The Welsh shires were not effectively incorporated in the English governmental system for another two hundred years, by which time a Welsh dynasty, the House of Tudor, was on the throne.

For a few months in the year 1290 Edward I believed he might secure the peaceful union of Britain by a marriage between the child-Queen of Scotland, Margaret, and his son, Edward of Caernarvon. Margaret, however, died in the Orkneys at the end of September 1290. Edward I claimed the right of arbitration between the rival aspirants for the Scottish throne, installed puppet governors in the Scottish lowlands, and carried off the traditional coronation stone from Scone to Westminster. By 1296 Edward was exacting oaths of loyalty from the bishops, earls and baronage of Scotland, as though he were himself sovereign north of the border. The Scots, like the Welsh, revolted. In William Wallace they found a patriotic resistance leader with a natural gift for guerrilla warfare. An English force was defeated at Stirling Bridge in May 1297 but in the following year Edward himself led a large army of English, Welsh and Gascons into Scotland and defeated Wallace at Falkirk – a battle in which, for the first time, the longbows of the English and Welsh archers proved decisive. The Scots, however, were not prepared to accept the direct rule of an English king. In March 1306 Robert Bruce, the head of one of the Scottish baronial families which claimed the throne, was crowned at Scone. Once again Edward set out to meet a challenge beyond the border. But the veteran of sixty-eight years and some twenty campaigns found the summer heat was too much for him. He died on the sands of Solway on 7 July 1307.

Edward I's last command was that his son and heir should carry his bones at the head of the English army until every Scottish soldier had been killed or captured. If this gesture was characteristic of the 'hammer of the Scots', it was no less characteristic of his son to disregard it. Edward II, then in his twenty-fourth year, was described by a chronicler as 'a prince fair of body and great of strength'. He was not a natural soldier; he liked minstrels and swimming and dressing-up; he liked, above all, Piers Gaveston, a good-looking Gascon who had been his close friend since childhood. Rather than prosecute his father's Scottish campaign, Edward II chose to return to London, where he prepared for his marriage to Isabella, daughter of King Philip IV of France. Gaveston was left as Regent while Edward crossed to Boulogne in January 1308 to marry his twelve-year-old bride. Subsequently the finest and most bejewelled wedding gifts were handed over by the King to Gaveston (who had been created Earl of Cornwall); and Gaveston was accorded precedence over all other subjects of the King at his coronation a month later.

Within a year of Edward I's death the English baronage, incensed by the young King's laziness and the favours shown to Gaveston, were seeking to impose restraints on their sovereign. And so they continued to do throughout his twenty-years' reign. Gaveston, excommunicated by the Archbishop of Canterbury and twice forced to flee the kingdom, was captured and executed in June 1312. Over the next ten years effective power was exercised by the King's first cousin, Thomas, who had appropriated for himself the five earldoms of Lancaster, Leicester, Derby, Lincoln and Salisbury. Although Thomas paid lip-service to the need for governmental reform (even speaking well of Parliaments) he was at heart a grasping and brutal over-mighty subject, with little interest in the realm as a whole. When, in 1314, Edward II sought at last to renew the war against the Scots, Thomas remained inactive. The campaign itself was disastrous. Robert Bruce, with a much smaller army, easily outmanoeuvred Edward, who was defeated at Bannockburn on 24 June 1314. The Scots invaded England and eventually captured Berwick, the

RIGHT France and England
united – for a time: the marriage
of Edward II and Isabella.

BELOW Berkeley Castle,
Gloucestershire, the scene of
Edward II's brutal murder in
1327.

A satirical comment on the downfall of Edward II, from the Holkham Bible picture book. The King is seen on a revolving wheel, grasping a crown, wearing it, losing it and finally without it.

key citadel built up by Edward I as a base for operations north of the border. The long-term significance of Bannockburn was to safeguard the independence of Scotland and postpone the union of the island for three centuries. The immediate effect was to confirm the power of the English magnate who had stayed at home, Thomas of Lancaster.

Edward learned nothing from his errors or misfortunes. He gave favours to two ambitious Marcher Lords, Hugh le Despenser and his son, who helped him to isolate and destroy the power of Thomas, captured and beheaded in March 1322. But the Despensers, too, aroused resentment among the nobility and were hated by Edward's queen Isabella. In 1325 Isabella went to Paris on a diplomatic mission for Edward II to her brother, the King of France. Yet once in Paris she began to intrigue with her lover, Roger Mortimer, Earl of March, an enemy of the Despensers. In September 1326 Isabella and Mortimer mounted an invasion of England, landed near Ipswich and were welcomed by a people weary of Edward and the Despensers. The royal favourites were rounded up and executed, the King himself imprisoned and deposed. In September 1327 Edward II was revoltingly murdered by agents of Mortimer in the dungeons of Berkeley Castle, a red-hot iron spit being thrust into his bowels.

Edward III, the fourteen-year-old son of Edward II and

Isabella, had been crowned at Westminster seven months before his father's murder. For the first three years of his reign he accepted the domination of Isabella and Mortimer and the nominal regency of a council of barons headed by Henry of Lancaster, the dead Thomas's younger brother. In 1330 Edward III successfully shed his leading strings. Mortimer was executed, but there was no widespread slaughter of his followers. Henry of Lancaster encouraged Edward to assert himself and then retired into private life. The disgraced Queen Mother – still only thirty-four – was pardoned, assigned an annual allowance of £3000, and lived on for twenty-eight more years at Castle Rising, in Norfolk. Her son was determined not to perpetuate the bitter feuding within the baronage, which was dangerous for the throne and the kingdom as a whole.

Outwardly he succeeded well enough. Edward III, like his grandfather, was a military commander of genius who understood the psychology of his barons-in-chief. But in half a century interests had changed. Edward I always hankered after the crusading ideal: Edward III substituted, for the unattainable Jerusalem, a knightly chivalry of jousts and tournaments in which pageantry, military prowess and courage could be displayed for the entertainment of a feudal society still primarily organized for war. Shared delight in watching the hazards of combat in the lists formed a bond linking king and baronage; and by 1344 the King had become so imbued with respect for the knightly virtues that he took a solemn oath to emulate King Arthur and found a Round Table for his knights. Four years later the Order of the Garter was established, a brotherhood of twenty-six knights 'co-partners both in Peace and War, assistant to one another in all serious and dangerous Exploits'. So long as the sovereign, as head of the Order, was himself a soldier of distinction, there was no risk of a relapse into the baronial anarchy of the previous reign.

England was at war for the greater part of Edward III's fifty years on the throne. The fighting, however, was spasmodic, with vigorous and bloody campaigns separated by long periods of truce or uneasy peace. At first the enemy was Scottish, and in 1332–3 Edward successfully restored the English ascendancy along the border which Bannockburn had toppled. But Edward's main interests lay across the Channel. In 1328 the death of his uncle, Charles IV, left France divided within itself. Charles IV had no male heir and there was opposition to the accession of his cousin, Philip IV of Valois. Edward III exploited this uncertain situation, maintaining that, through his mother, he had a good claim to the French throne. In picking a quarrel with France at this time Edward had three objectives: recovery of the lost Angevin lands; destruction of the strategically dangerous alliance between the French and the Scots; and the protection of the English wool merchants' interests,

ABOVE An illustration from the *Canterbury Tales* by Chaucer, who was writing at a time when English was superseding French as the official language.

OPPOSITE The head of the effigy of Edward II, from his tomb in Gloucester Cathedral.

which seemed menaced by French expansion towards the Flemish manufacturing towns. For Edward's barons the prime attraction of war across the Channel was the opportunity to plunder the richest kingdom in Europe.

Yet the first stage of what was to become known as the Hundred Years War proved disappointing for the English. In June 1340 the naval victory of Sluys gratified the merchants by safeguarding communications with Flanders, but there were scant rewards for the baronage. Suddenly in the summer of 1346 the character of the war changed. Edward III landed in Normandy and his knights and soldiery ravaged the countryside between the Seine and the Somme before being brought to battle by Philip VI at Crécy on 26 August. Although the French outnumbered Edward's army by nearly five to one, the accuracy, range and rapid fire of the English longbows revolutionized battle tactics. The French cavalry was halted by shower upon shower of arrows. Casualties were astonishingly high. Edward followed up this momentous victory at Crécy with an advance on Calais, which he besieged. When, in August 1347, Calais surrendered, it provided the rulers of England with a continental foothold that they retained for another two hundred years.

ABOVE The seal of Edward III.   BELOW Edward III instructs builders engaged in constructing the Abbey at St Albans.

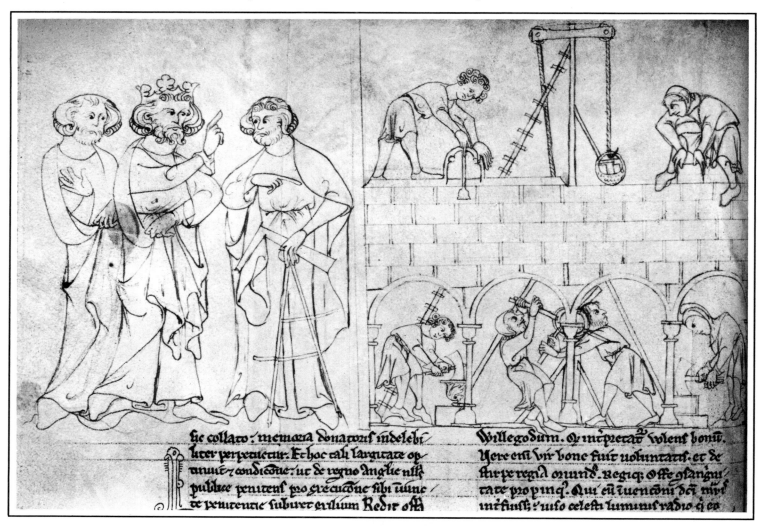

LEFT The battle of Crècy, 1346, one of the major confrontations in the Hundred Years' War, was a triumph for the English Longbowmen. From Froissart's *Chronicles*.

BELOW Edward III attacks the Scots.

The legendary six burghers of Calais plead with Edward III to spare the citizens after the town has fallen to him.

There followed a lull lasting for nearly a decade. In 1350 Philip VI was succeeded by his son, John 'the Good'. There was a change of generation, too, among the principal English combatants. Edward III's renown was soon challenged by his son, the Black Prince, who had fought at Crécy as a lad of sixteen. The Black Prince, acting as lieutenant-governor of Gascony, won booty and notoriety by plundering the Mediterranean provinces of France in 1355–6. More remarkably, on 19 September 1356, he succeeded in defeating John the Good at Poitiers and taking him prisoner. Possession of the French King in person enabled Edward III to conclude a favourable treaty at Bretigny in 1360: nearly a quarter of the French kingdom, including the whole of Aquitaine, was ceded to the English.

It would have been better for Edward III's reputation had he succumbed to the plague which ravaged England's French possessions in 1361. For the last sixteen years of his life were marked by frustrations. The French found in Bertrand du Guesclin an enterprising General able to liberate French lands whose peoples were smarting under the harsh administration of Edward's sons. The Black Prince captured du Guesclin at Najera in 1367 but did not destroy either his army or his reputation. Neither he nor his father could check the French and by 1376 Edward III had lost all his conquests, except for Calais and a narrow strip of coastal lands in south-western France.

In England, too, Edward's final years were marked by humiliations. Popular discontent with heavy taxation and the alleged greed of the King's principal ministers led to sustained criticism of the Court and its expenditure by the Parliaments of 1371, 1372, 1373 and, above all, by the so-called 'Good Parliament' of 1376. These attacks on the government – which, in 1376, involved the impeachment of several royal officials – were a clear sign that the political initiative was, once again, passing away from the crown. Despite the chivalric pageantry of his years of triumph, Edward III left the monarchy no stronger than he found it.

4
Struggle for the Throne 1377~1485

RICHARD II is the most tragic figure among the crowned rulers of medieval England. His accession, at the age of ten, came only a year after the death of his awe-inspiring father, the Black Prince. It was hard for the boy to measure up to his father's legend. Nor was this the only unwelcome legacy from his grandfather's reign. Young Richard's court was overshadowed by his three royal ducal uncles: Edmund of Langley (Duke of York); Thomas of Woodstock (Duke of Gloucester); and, above all, the powerful John of Gaunt (Duke of Lancaster). These mightiest of subjects and their offspring began a power struggle for the throne which disrupted English society for more than a century.

At first, however, it seemed as if the principal threat came from the lower orders rather than from the feudal baronage. In 1381 Richard was faced by the astonishing crisis of the Peasants' Revolt, when the people of Essex and Kent refused to pay the newfangled poll-tax and swept rebelliously on London. The courage shown by the young King before the mob at Mile End and Smithfield was impressive. The rioters showed respect for their sovereign's pledged word. From these dramatic happenings young Richard learnt that, for most of his subjects, monarchy possessed a mystical quality worthy of reverence. Small wonder if, in later years. Richard II faced the challenge of baronial opposition by proclaiming a divine right of kingship.

LEFT Richard II was a relatively cultured king, who appreciated the finer things of life. Here he presides over a royal banquet.

OPPOSITE A contemporary artist's imaginary conception of Richard II abdicating in favour of Henry IV.

Richard II is escorted to the Tower of London by soldiers. Shortly afterwards he was moved to Pontefract Castle, where he died in very suspicious circumstances.

Both Richard and his opponents thought frequently of the follies and fate of his great-grandfather, Edward II. Twice at least Richard urged the Pope to canonize Edward. Yet there was no real parallel between the two kings. Richard was a patron of the arts, a cultured ruler sensitive to fashion – he is the first English king known to have possessed a handkerchief. He was loyal to friends who shared his interests and who, like him, preferred diplomacy to war. Whereas Edward II had been weak in character, Richard was self-assertive. In 1387 the Duke of Gloucester and four other prominent peers (including John of Gaunt's son, the future Henry IV) began a brief civil war to remove the King's favourites from what they regarded as an effeminately civilized court. They succeeded all too well. With the backing of the 'Merciless Parliament' of 1388, these five magnates – the Lords Appellant, as they were called – established themselves as effective custodians of the land. For the next decade Richard concentrated on building up a reputation for good government, skilfully seeking to free himself from dependence upon the Lords Appellant. If he thought of taking revenge on them, he was in no hurry to exact it.

There is much to be said in favour of Richard's states-manship during the early 1390s. He reached a settlement with France and he visited Ireland, where he had some success in rationalizing the government of an anarchic people resentful of any alien ascendancy. To these years, too, belong his encouragement of the arts – his patronage of portrait painting, his friendship with Geoffrey Chaucer, his interest in the building of Westminster Hall. But in 1394 the death of his much-loved Queen, Anne of Bohemia, destroyed the balance of his temperament. By 1397 he had become pathologically suspicious of plots. He raised a private army, retainers wearing his crest of the white hart, and recruited in Ireland, Wales and Cheshire, where he believed men were loyal to him. With these retainers he struck at last against the Lords Appellant. His uncle Gloucester was arrested and murdered; one of the Earls executed; and the three remaining Appellants eventually exiled. At the same time Richard sought to make himself an absolute monarch, exacting from Parliament a grant of revenue for life and confiscating the property and lands of his enemies.

But Richard made two fatal mistakes. On John of Gaunt's death in 1388 he ordered his estate to be forfeit to the crown rather than to pass to his son, Henry Boling-broke, one of the exiled Lords Appellant. And, having thus afforded a just grievance to a strong claimant to the throne, Richard then departed for Ireland where his earlier success was endangered by a nationalistic uprising. Less than five weeks after Richard's arrival in Ireland, Henry Boling-broke mustered enough forces to cross from France and land at the mouth of the Humber. There, in the King's absence, it was easy enough for Henry to raise 'all the people of the north country' against Richard's alleged tyranny. By the time Richard hurried back from Ireland, he found himself isolated and without support. The House of Lancaster had usurped the throne. On 13 October 1399 Henry IV was crowned at Westminster, with the fallen King three miles down river, imprisoned in the Tower of London. Four months later, still in custody, Richard died mysteriously at Pontefract. No one knows if he was stabbed, poisoned or starved to death.

Yet Henry IV, backed by Church and Parliament, had won his throne too easily. His prime concern was to secure what he had usurped. During his first nine years on the throne he was faced with five rebellious movements. If one feudal magnate could appropriate the crown of England, there was no reason why other powerful barons, linked together by family connections and territorial interests, should not further the fortunes of their own dynasties. There was nothing constructive in his reign. Year after year he concentrated on warding off danger, real or imaginary : from the northern baronage ; from Wales, where Owen Glendower rekindled the flame of patriotic resistance; from Scotland, which afforded sanctuary to those who rebelled against Henry ; from heretics questioning the authority of the Church, which had backed his dynastic claims; and from within his own council where, from 1411 onwards, his eldest son had strong champions. For Henry IV, a neurotic hypochondriac, was far from popular. The younger barons, together with the merchant class, wished to resume the war with the French, who were constantly encroaching on England's trading interests. But Henry, prematurely aged, would not commit the country to a military expedition which he could not himself lead.

He died, a few weeks short of his forty-seventh birthday, in March 1413. His son, Henry V, was a bachelor of twenty-five with an appearance so impressive that chroniclers felt a need to describe him : tall and athletic, with a long neck, high cheekbones, thick brown hair cropped like a priest, and large brown eyes. Already much of his life had been spent on campaigns in England and Wales, and he had every intention of reviving the dubious claims of Edward III to the French throne. Yet before he could embark on war he was faced by two serious conspiracies : early in 1414 the Protestant heretics known as Lollards attempted to seize the King and the city of London ; while a year later a plot was discovered at Southampton to assassinate all four sons of Henry IV, replacing Henry V by a claimant nominated by the anti-Lancastrian faction. The ringleaders of the Southampton plot – men close to the King at court – were executed. So long as the war with France prospered, there were no further threats to the throne from the great

baronial families. But the problem of the over-mighty subject remained unresolved.

Henry V sailed from the Solent with an invasion fleet of fifteen hundred vessels in the second week of August 1415. Harfleur was besieged and taken, but the army was weakened by dysentry. Rather than risk an assault on Paris, Henry turned northwards towards the Somme and Calais. On 25 October the French attacked the English at Agincourt, eighteen miles north of Crécy. The French rashly attempted a cavalry charge on a position in a muddy defile three-quarters of a mile wide and manned by eight thousand longbowmen. In less than three hours fighting they lost some six thousand men.

The victory of Agincourt made Henry V a legendary warrior king. So long as he was in the field, the French had no wish for pitched battles. But it took many months of siege warfare to secure the mastery of Normandy which Henry had set as his first objective. In 1419, before he had completed this task, he gained a diplomatic triumph. Internal quarrels within France enabled him to detach the Burgundians from their alliance with the French and, at the same time, to have himself recognized as Regent of the French kingdom. The treaty of Troyes of May 1420 provided that he should marry Catherine of Valois, daughter

of the imbecile French king, who would recognize Henry as his heir. The marriage was celebrated the following month and, in December 1421, a son was born at Windsor. It was assumed that, in the fullness of time, the boy would become King of England and of France. But his accession came sooner than anyone anticipated, for in the following summer Henry contracted dysentery, while besieging Meaux. Thirty-eight weeks after Catherine had given birth to their son, Henry V was dead.

The accession of the infant Henry VI was a major political misfortune for the English: it prevented consolidation of Henry V's successes in France; and it made inevitable a resumption of the power struggle for possession of the throne. Henry VI himself, even when he grew to manhood, was a pitiable figure. Although crowned at Westminster in November 1429 and again, as nominal King of France, at Notre Dame in Paris five months later, Henry was never more than a saintly pawn in the game of power politics. He hated all bloodshed and prayed sincerely for peace at home and abroad. His two magnificent foundations, at Eton and King's College, Cambridge, preserve the memory of a sovereign who would rather have been a priest or even a friar.

Meanwhile, in the heart of France, a different set of

OPPOSITE The coronation of
Henry IV, from Froissart's
Chronicles.

RIGHT The victor of Agin-
court – Henry V, the warrior
king who regained much of
England's prestige and added to
her possessions in France.

saintly qualities enabled Joan of Arc to stir the patriotism of her countrymen. Henry VI's ministers and military commanders had no answer to the revived fighting spirit of the French. For the first twenty years of the reign Henry's great-uncle, Cardinal Beaufort, Bishop of Winchester, retained considerable influence over policy, while the Cardinal's nephews, John and Edmund, commanded armies in France. The Cardinal was so wealthy that he made substantial loans to the Exchequer, always at high rates of interest, and on one occasion with the crown jewels surrendered as security. The Beauforts were understandably unpopular. So too was the King's favourite, the Duke of Suffolk, who in 1444 arranged an incongruous marriage, binding holy Henry to the fiery and passionate Margaret of Anjou, a vixen of fifteen. Six years later Suffolk's enemies had little difficulty in persuading Parliament to impeach him for embezzlement, and he was murdered while in custody. Public feeling was turning against the whole Lancastrian establishment which had embarked on a French war it was unable to win. The Court seemed to live lavishly – apart, that is, from the King – but, despite heavy taxation, the common soldiers remained unpaid. Small wonder that, in 1450, a rising known after its leader as 'Jack Cade's Rebellion' threatened royal London and Westminster.

Continued on pg 64

LEFT The affluent medieval society. Heavy taxation, fixed wages and the restraints of the feudal system all influenced the aggrieved peasants to revolt against the upper classes when incited by Wat Tyler and others.

BELOW John Ball riding in front of the peasants, who bear the standards of England and St George.

THE PEASANTS' REVOLT

In June 1381 mob rule triumphed briefly in London for the first time in the capital's history. For the past thirty years there had been unrest among the agricultural workers: villeins resented the restraints of feudal bondage; free labourers hated statutes imposed to hold down wages in the economic turmoil which followed the Black Death. These grievances were intensified by the imposition of a Poll Tax in 1380 to pay for a war with France which dragged on unsuccessfully and was therefore unpopular. Peasant revolts had already taken place in several European countries earlier in the century, the most famous being the French *Jacquerie* of 1358, after the Black Prince's victory at Poitiers. What distinguishes the English revolt from its continental counterparts is its attitude to the Church as an institution.

The revolt began with a refusal to pay taxes in Essex. It spread across the Thames Estuary to Kent where a rebellious crowd chose as their leader a skilled artisan, Walter the Tiler, 'Wat Tyler' as they called him. The Kentish crowd carried all before them in Rochester and Maidstone and marched on Canterbury. There they released from jail a radical excommunicated priest, John Ball. He had not been content like other preachers merely to denounce wealth and pride but encouraged the peasantry to take violent action against the social order, both in Church and State. With Tyler and Ball as their leaders the Kentish rebels advanced to Blackheath and the Essex rebels to Mile End.

On Thursday, 13 June, Tyler's men ran amok south of the Thames, devastated Southwark, burnt the Archbishop's home at Lambeth, then rushed across the river and sacked John of Gaunt's palace of the Savoy. Next day the fourteen-year-old Richard II bravely faced the Essex mob at Mile End, promising them the abolition of villeinage, an end to wage restraint for labour services, and pardon. Many Essex men then went home, but Tyler's followers burst into the Tower of London and dragged out the Archbishop of Canterbury (Simon of Sudbury) from his prayers. The Archbishop and three companions were beheaded on Tower Hill. On Saturday, 15 June, a royal official was seized in the sanctuary of Westminster Abbey and executed in the City; but when a confrontation between Tyler and Richard II at Smithfield looked dangerous, the Lord Mayor seized and stabbed Tyler, while the King called on the mob to follow him out northwards from London.

Once order was restored in the capital, the rebels had no chance of success. Outrages continued, particularly at the abbeys of St Albans and Bury St Edmunds as well as in Norwich. Pledges given under duress at Mile End were not honoured. Most of the surviving rebel spokesmen were executed. But the revolt was not a total failure. Nothing more was heard of the poll tax, and the emancipation of serfs from villeinage continued gradually over the next two or three generations. Yet the principal lesson of 1381 was a warning for the higher clergy. Excessive wealth and political power were dissolving peasant piety. Pilgrims might still kneel for the martyred Becket; they shed no tears for the murdered Sudbury.

ABOVE Cold feet and chilblains were an occupational hazard of the medieval peasant, out in all weathers.
RIGHT Confrontation at Smithfield. On the right, the young Richard II addresses the mob, while on the left he watches as Wat Tyler is killed by the Lord Mayor of London.

The alternative to Lancastrian rule was not, however, a democratic movement: it was a shift in loyalty to the baronial faction headed by Richard, Duke of York. He was descended both from John of Gaunt's elder brother (through his mother) and from Gaunt's younger brother (through his father, who was executed after the Southampton plot of 1415). The Duke was an efficient military commander and the richest landowner in the kingdom, capable of raising an enormous private army of retainers. His opportunity came in 1453. For in August that year Henry VI's mind became dulled: periodically he was paralysed in speech and incapable of any recognized mental activity. The forceful Queen Margaret sought the power of a Regent for herself; Parliament favoured Richard of York. There lay the principal cause of the final series of conflicts between the great baronial houses. It is this contest – a struggle involving the feudal magnates and their retainers throughout the land – to which, three and a half centuries later, Sir Walter Scott gave the misleadingly romantic name of 'the Wars of the Roses'.

These baronial wars continued intermittently from 1455 to 1485, with some sixteen encounters which are generally rated as battles. Richard of York was killed in the third of these engagements, the battle of Wakefield at the end of December 1460; but within eleven weeks his eldest son had entered London in strength and was acclaimed King Edward IV. Margaret, with the luckless Henry VI in her camp, was defeated at Towton on 29 March 1461, the biggest and bloodiest battle of all, fought in a Yorkshire snowstorm on Palm Sunday. Henry and Margaret fled northwards and found sanctuary across the border in Edinburgh. Edward IV returned to London and was crowned on midsummer's day.

The Yorkists had promised just and orderly government at home and a vigorous policy abroad. But, though Edward did much to combat brigandage and make England a land fit for merchants to trade in, he could not fulfil the Yorkist reform programme. He had come to the throne with the backing of the last powerful territorial magnate, the 'kingmaker' Earl of Warwick (son of his mother's brother). The Earl wanted to determine foreign policy and to advance the fortunes of his own family. But, once on the throne, Edward showed independence of mind. He ignored Warwick's initiative in foreign affairs and married, not a foreign princess chosen by Warwick, but the beautiful Lady Elizabeth Woodville, widow of one of the Lancastrian barons. Warwick duly renewed the armed struggle in 1469. For a time he even forced Edward into exile in Holland and Flanders, and Henry VI was restored to the throne. But the Lancastrian leaders – especially Margaret of Anjou – did not trust Warwick. Edward's standing abroad was high enough for him to fit out an expedition; and it

ABOVE Drawing of Henry V's forces besieging Rouen during his French campaigns.

OPPOSITE Richard Beauchamp is made master of the infant Henry VI, only nine months old at his accession.

64

Here shewes howe acordyng to the last wille of kyng hem the 6th Erle Richard
by the auctorite of the hole pleament was master to kyng hem the 6th And
so he contynued til the tyme kyng was xxj yere of age And then ffyrst by
his great labour he was dischardged

Henry VI was a pious, saintly scholar in an age which demanded strong, forceful rulers. By 1453 only Calais remained of his father Henry V's French conquests.

proved comparatively easy for the Yorkists to divide their opponents and defeat them separately. Warwick was killed at the battle of Barnet in April 1471. Three weeks later the Lancastrian cause seemed irretrievably lost when Margaret was defeated at Tewkesbury and the only son of her marriage to Henry perished in the fighting.

Henry VI himself had fallen into Edward's hands on the eve of Barnet. He was murdered in the Tower of London on the night following Edward's return from Tewkesbury. There was a ruthless quality in Edward's character, inevitable in a kingdom where terror was the true instrument of government. In 1478 Edward consigned his brother the Duke of Clarence to the Tower, for suspected treason; and there Clarence met his death, being drowned either in a bath or (as a contemporary declared) in a barrel of Malmsey wine. His fate was a dire warning to any feudal lord seeking to restart the cycle of rebellion.

Edward IV was an English prototype of the Renaissance prince. Like his grandson Henry VIII, Edward was in his youth sharp-witted and high-spirited; and, again like Henry, he seemed massive in his armour, for he was over six feet tall and broad-shouldered. As well as being a good soldier and an astute diplomat, Edward knew how to satisfy the interests of the City of London and its merchants. Probably chroniclers exaggerate the permissiveness of his Court in contrast to Henry IV's personal austerity, but there is no doubt he was by nature libidinous. He delighted in the company of several low-born mistresses, openly extending protection to their husbands and dependents by royal letters-patent. His best known love was Jane Shore, wife of a London mercer: 'Where the King took displeasure she would mitigate and appease his mind, and where men were out of favour, she would bring them into his grace', a contemporary wrote. Yet not all Edward's pursuit of pleasure was frivolously self-indulgent. Again like the Italian Renaissance princes, he encouraged the arts and learning. The protector of Jane Shore was also the patron of William Caxton, whose printing press was set up at Westminster in 1476.

Yet Edward did not redeem the Yorkists' promise of good, stable government. He neither strengthened the executive nor brought the nobility to heel. When he died, in April 1483, the power struggle resumed with new contestants. Edward's will appointed his youngest brother Richard, Duke of Gloucester, as Protector of his heir, the twelve-year-old Edward V. But the Woodvilles and the Greys – the child's mother's family – provoked violence by attempting to exclude Richard and hurry through Edward V's coronation. Richard, in his turn, secured custody of young Edward and his ten-year-old brother. They were removed to the Tower of London, from which neither of them ever emerged. Richard officially questioned

ABOVE Henry VI's greatest achievements were probably the foundation of Eton and King's College, Cambridge. The Chapel at King's is a masterpiece of English Perpendicular architecture.

LEFT Edward IV with the beautiful Elizabeth Woodville, whom he married against the advice of Warwick the king-maker, who wanted a useful foreign alliance, and their son Edward.

Fol. xxb.

The tragical doynges of Kyng Richard the thirde.

LOthe I am to remembre, but more I abhore to write, the miserable tragedy of this infortunate prince, which by fraude entered, by tyrannye proceded, and by sodayn deathe ended his infortunate life: But yf I should not declare the flagicious factes of the euyll princes, aswell as I haue done the notable actes of vertuous kinges, I shoulde neither animate, nor incourage rulers of royalmes, Countreyes and Seigniories to folowe the steppes of their profitable progenitors, for to attayne to the type of honour and worldly fame: neither yet aduertise princes being proane to vice and wickednes, to aduoyde and expell all synne and mischiefe, for dread of obloquy and worldly shame: for contrary set to contrary is more apparaunt, as whyte ioyned with black, maketh the fayrer shewe: Wherfore, I will procede in his actes after my accustomed vsage.

RICHARD the third of that name, vsurped ye croune of Englad & openly toke vpon hym to bee kyng, the nyntene date of June, in the yere of our lord.a thousand foure hundred lxxiii.and in the.xxb.yere of Lewes the leuenth then beeyng French kyng:and the morow after, he was proclaymed kyng and with great solempnite rode to Westminster, and there sate in the seate roial, and called before him the iudges of ye realme straightely commaundynge them to execute the lawe with out fauoure or delaie, with many good exhortaciõs(of the which he folowed not one) and then he departed towarde the Abbaye, and at the churche dooze he was mett with procession, and by the abbot to hym was deliuered the scepter of saincte Edwarde, and so went and offered to saincte Edwarde his shrine, while the Monkes sang Te deum with a faint courage, and from the churche he returned to the palaice, where he lodged till the coronacion. And to be sure of all enemies(as he thoughte)he sent for fiue thousand men of the North againft his coronaciõ, whiche came vp euil appareled and worse harneissed, in rusty harneys, neither defensable nor skoured to the sale, whiche mustered in Finesbury felde, to the great disdain of all the lookers on.

The fourth daie of July he came to the tower by water with his wife, and the fifth daie he created Edward his onely begotten sonne, a childe of.x.yere olde, prince of wales, and Jhon haward, a man of great knowlege and vertue (aswell in counsaill as in battaill) he created Duke of
EE.i.   Norffolke

the validity of Edward IV's marriage and his children were declared illegitimate. A commission from the 'lords and commons of England' then offered Richard the throne. Twelve weeks after Edward IV's death he was crowned in the presence of nearly all the peerage, whom he subsequently entertained to a five-hour banquet in Westminster.

Richard III has the reputation of an arch-villain among England's rulers. Even his physical appearance has been distorted, a frail frame with one shoulder higher than the other becoming 'crouchback' of legend and Shakespeare. Although his guilt remains unproven, it is probable he was responsible for the murder of the 'two princes in the Tower', as Tudor propagandists maintained. There is some evidence, from Yorkshire, that he was an able and diligent administrator with a sense of justice for the common

people, if not for the baronage. But his two-year reign was one long rearguard action, in which he sought to fend off new treasons and forestall a cross-Channel invasion by the sole Lancastrian claimant, Henry Tudor.

Ultimately Richard III failed. Henry landed, not in England, but on the Pembrokeshire coast at Milford Haven. Richard fought courageously, although faced with desertions. In the mêlée, he was struck down, the only sovereign of England to be killed in battle after the Norman Conquest. The crown was placed on the head of the Welshman, Henry Tudor. It is one of history's ironies that the victor of the long baronial struggle should have been a man who, until the very morning of Bosworth, had never heard the thud of cannon balls or seen archers bend their bows in anger.

5
Tudor Magnificence 1485~1603

WHEN early in September 1485 Henry VII rode into London, he hardly knew the kingdom he had won at Bosworth. Half of his twenty-eight years were spent in Wales, the remainder in Brittany. Only once before had he visited Westminster. In November 1470 he was received by Henry VI, temporarily back on the throne by sufferance of Warwick. On that occasion the King surprised his courtiers by predicting that eventually the young Welshman would triumph over both the Lancastrians and their adversaries. It seemed unlikely then, and scarcely more probable a year later when, after Tewkesbury, the direct Lancastrian line became extinct. For dynastically Henry Tudor was a rank outsider. His grandmother was Henry VI's mother who, after Henry V's death, secretly married a minor official at court, Owen Tudor, from Anglesey. Their second son, whom his royal half-brother created Earl of Richmond, married Lady Margaret Beaufort, a great-granddaughter of John of Gaunt; and in January 1457 the thirteen-year-old Lady Margaret, by now two months a widow, gave birth to Henry Tudor at Pembroke Castle. Even after the killings of the baronial wars, there were still in 1485 some ten claimants with a better title to the crown than Henry VII, among them his mother.

He gained the throne, and retained it for twenty-four years, as much through intelligence and astuteness as through the exercise of kingly rights or qualities. Early in 1486 he married Elizabeth of York, the eldest of Edward IV's children, a tall and elegant blonde of twenty. The marriage was intended to spike Yorkist counter-claims and to hold out a prospect of reconciliation. But it did not, in itself, rule out a renewal of the baronial struggles. He had to thwart the plots of pretenders and, above all, to make central government so effective that a feudal baron could no longer maintain an army of his own.

Two Yorkist pretenders, Lambert Simnel and Perkin Warbeck, were backed by Edward IV's sister, Margaret of Burgundy, and supported by dissident members of the old nobility. Simnel, who was the son of an Oxfordshire tradesman, was represented as the heir to the Duke of Clarence. He crossed from Ireland with 2000 German mercenaries and landed in Lancashire in the summer of 1487. Henry VII had to muster an army larger than the force he had commanded at Bosworth in order to defeat Simnel, fighting a pitched battle south of Newark. Perkin Warbeck, who claimed to be the younger prince imprisoned by Richard III in the Tower, troubled Henry intermittently from 1493 to 1499, not least because the rulers of France and Scotland used him as a tiresome pawn in their diplomatic calculations. So long as it was faced by such emergencies the Tudor dynasty could not be secure on the throne.

But Henry's best guarantee of stability was sound administration. There was nothing revolutionary in his concept of government. Basically he used the same administrative machinery as his predecessors, but he overhauled it. The old aristocratic names disappeared from the King's Council, which was given new teeth with laws against retainers and private armies, and with an intimidating Court of Star Chamber to impose the royal will impartially on all Henry's subjects. Central power was spread downwards and outwards by reforming and extending the local duties of the Justices of the Peace, an office created in the late twelfth century but only becoming the chief agency of local government under the Tudors. Henceforth the power of the nobility over the countryside was offset by the authority of the sovereign's magistrates, recruited like all Henry's advisers from the professions or from the small landowning gentry (the very class among whom the Tudors themselves originated).

There was nothing glamorous in Henry VII's personality. He has never warmed the prose of historians. Like Edward IV, he was interested in trade and in securing favourable terms for the English merchants abroad. Unlike Edward, he was thrifty by nature, determined to make the monarchy solvent and insisting on auditing accounts himself. He encouraged his friend and Chancellor, Cardinal Morton (who was also Archbishop of Canterbury) to raise substantial

Edward, Prince of Wales and
Richard, Duke of York, from
a stained glass window in
Canterbury Cathedral.

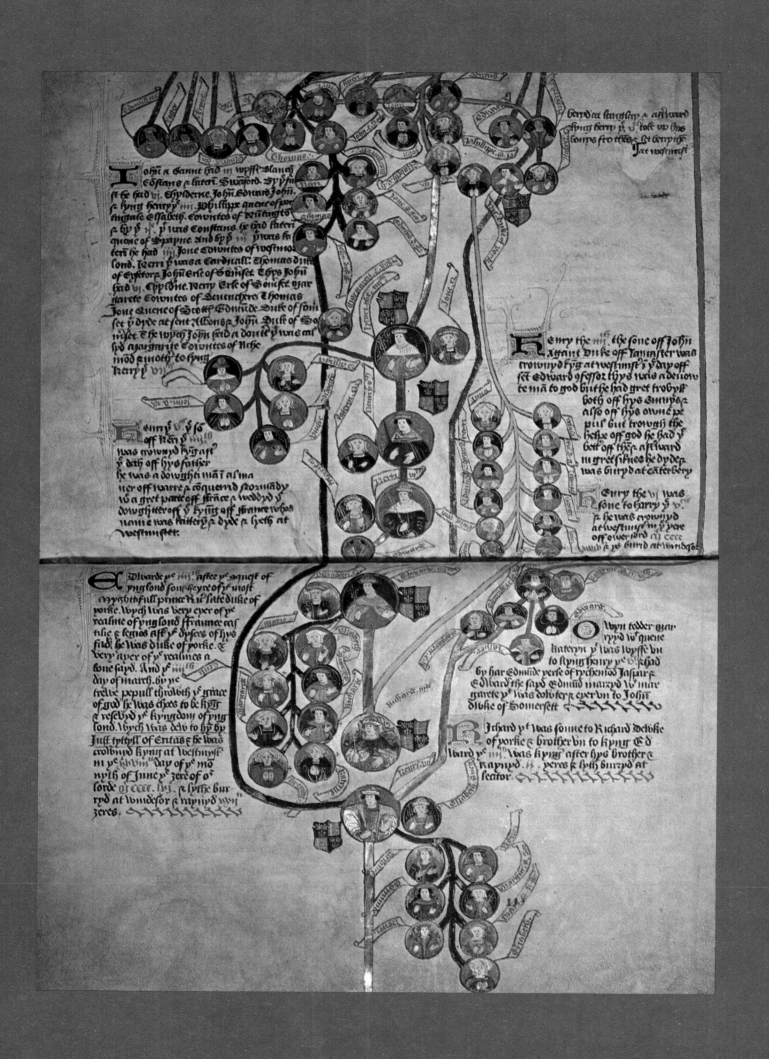

OPPOSITE The genealogy of Henry VII, showing his rather haphazard descent from John of Gaunt.

RIGHT Lady Margaret Beaufort, great-granddaughter of John of Gaunt and mother of Henry Tudor.

BELOW It took the Lancastrian-supported victor of Bosworth, Henry Tudor – subsequently Henry VII – to marry into the House of York and bring much-needed peace and order to England.

forced loans ('benevolences') and is partly responsible for the ingenious dilemma known as 'Morton's Fork': if a subject liable for taxation lived opulently, he was clearly wealthy enough to pay a royal benevolence; and if he lived austerely, then he was growing rich by his economies and could pay the benevolence just the same. Cardinal Morton was far from popular, and even more detested were the unscrupulous privy councillors, Empson and Dudley, who applied Morton's Fork. Yet between them they saw to it that the crown, heavily in debt in 1485, ended the reign with a credit balance of a million and a half pounds in the privy purse. Moreover, Henry VII personally was no miser: he had built Richmond Palace, and his chapel at West-minster Abbey remains testimony to his artistic good taste. Foreign envoys commented on the sumptuous banquets he would give, though it is probable that he regarded them as sound political investments, giving proof abroad of the outward magnificence of Tudor government.

Certainly Henry VII restored England's prestige in Europe. His marriage policy is significant: there were no unions of his children to the baronage; one daughter married the King of France, another the King of Scotland, while his eldest son Arthur married Catherine of Aragon, daughter of the joint sovereign of Spain. Arthur died of consumption five months after the marriage, but Henry VII was reluctant to abandon the Spanish connection, and

Henry VIII in his handsome, self-assured youth. Opposite are the famous and tragic six wives: (from the top, left to right) Catherine of Aragon, Anne Boleyn (mother of the future Elizabeth I), Jane Seymour (mother of the future Edward VI), Anne of Cleves, Catherine Howard and Catherine Parr.

Catherine was duly betrothed to his second son, the future Henry VIII. But Henry VII's health was too frail for him to see this wedding. He died at Richmond in April 1509. Henry VIII's marriage was celebrated six weeks later.

In Europe as a whole Henry VIII was to become the most notorious of English kings, the sovereign who broke loose from Rome, twice changing wives at the drop of an axe. But for the first half of his reign Henry was as conventional and orthodox as any other contemporary ruler. After participating as an ally of Spain in a brief campaign in France (1513), he tended to leave the direction of affairs to the able and ambitious diplomat, Thomas Wolsey, who became Archbishop of York in 1514 and a Cardinal and Lord Chancellor a year later. Wolsey was the effective ruler of England until the summer of 1529, thrusting his sovereign forward as the arbiter between the great European rivals, France and Spain. His foreign policy was brilliant, showy and expensive. At midsummer 1520 Wolsey stage-managed the 'Field of the Cloth of Gold', four weeks of jousts, banquets. summit talks and entertainments for Henry VIII and Francis I of France at Balinghem, eight miles south of Calais. This famous meeting was not politically productive; but it enabled Henry VIII to project on the Continent his favourite image – handsome, scholarly, a good linguist, a superb horseman, unrivalled in field sports and the martial arts, and an able musician. As if these qualities were not enough, in 1521 he added to them by becoming the first English king to be author of a printed book, *In Defence of the Seven Sacraments*, a tract exposing the heresies of the German Protestant, Martin Luther. The book was dedicated to Pop Leo X, who accorded Henry VIII a title borne by his successors down to the present day, 'Defender of the Faith'.

Catherine of Aragon had given birth to a son in 1511, but the prince lived only six weeks. There followed a succession of miscarriages and stillbirths, although Princess Mary (born in February 1516) seemed reasonably healthy. But by 1527 Henry VIII had convinced himself that the Almighty denied him a male heir because he had committed the sin of marrying his deceased brother's widow and he wished Wolsey to secure a papal annulment of his marriage. While negotiations continued between London and Rome, Henry became infatuated with Anne Boleyn, the twenty-year-old daughter of a former Lord Mayor, and wished to marry her. But Pope Clement, who was virtually under the control of Catherine's nephew, Emperor Charles V, was disinclined to oblige Wolsey or his master.

The 'King's Great Matter' – Henry's intention to separate from Catherine and marry Anne Boleyn – dominated politics for five years at a time when there was already a strongly nationalistic feeling towards the papacy and its representatives in England. People resented the heavy taxes

imposed by Cardinal Morton and Cardinal Wolsey, and readily blamed the Church rather than the King for the financial burdens they had to bear. Wolsey's failure in the 'Great Matter' led to his fall in 1529 and the advancement of a new chief minister, Thomas Cromwell, who advised Henry VIII that a formal breach with the Pope would allow the primate of England, Archbishop Thomas Cranmer, to declare the marriage with Catherine null and void. Under Thomas Cromwell's management, the Reformation Parliament of 1529–36 was sympathetic to the King's quarrel. It attacked the 'privileges of Rome' and the separate jurisdiction of the Church; it recognized Henry's secret marriage to Anne Boleyn of January 1533; and it declared the King to be Supreme Head of the Church in England. In 1536 and 1539 the monastic foundations were dissolved, the lands bringing great revenue to the crown. By selling the lands at comparatively cheap prices to his loyal servants, Henry VIII created a vested interest in the Tudor dynasty and the Reformation, to which his whims and caprices had given a characteristically English pattern.

While England was thus experiencing the greatest transference of land since the Norman Conquest, the King's matrimonial affairs vacillated between the tragic and the absurd. In September 1533 Anne Boleyn gave birth to Princess Elizabeth at Greenwich, but she failed to provide Henry with a male heir. The King gradually convinced himself that Anne had other lovers. On 19 May 1536 she was executed on trumped-up charges of treason in the Tower of London. Eleven days later Henry married Jane Seymour, the modest daughter of a Wiltshire knight. Jane did, indeed, provide him with a son (later Edward VI) in October 1537 but, to Henry's sorrow, she did not survive the confinement. Henry then remained a widower for over two years until in January 1540 he allowed himself – largely on the strength of a Holbein portrait – to contract a politically opportune marriage with Anne of Cleves, a plain-featured German princess who spoke no English and lacked courtly grace. The marriage was dissolved, unconsummated, six months later, in time for Henry to wed Catherine Howard, a cousin of Anne Boleyn, on 28 July the same year. She, however, was even more indiscreet than her cousin and suffered a similar fate in February 1542. Rather surprisingly, in the following year Henry found a sixth wife in the intellectually formidable Catherine Parr. She had already outlasted two husbands and she successfully survived the last phase of the King's life, a disconcerting four years in which the once handsome prince became an obese and querulous domestic tyrant.

Henry VIII lived in a Europe changing more rapidly than ever before. Discoveries were turning the attention of the Continent away from the Mediterranean to the oceans at a time when intellectual curiosity had begun to question the

bases of the medieval world and its conventions. Social and
religious revolution was in the air during the first decades
of his reign. It was Henry's achievement that, in England,
the revolutionary changes were imposed from above. The
principal crisis of his reign – the Pilgrimage of Grace of
1536 – was a rising in favour of old loyalties and familiar
ways, a conservative demonstration; and characteristically
Henry decided that the protest showed the need for
strengthening royal authority in the north. Like his father,
he sought sound administration through a council dominated, in the second half of the reign, by his will; but he
carried conciliar government geographically further than
Henry VII had done. Wales and the northern counties were

subjected to rule from London. The crown, partnered by
the lawyers and gentry in parliament, created a nation-
state. Henry VIII was a cruel and selfish realist in politics,
arrogantly flaunting the magnificence of his own majesty.
Yet he mirrored the growing pride and prosperity of his
subjects.

Henry VIII was succeeded by his frail son, Edward VI, a
precocious boy of nine who died of tuberculosis in July
1553, three months short of his sixteenth birthday. The
first part of his reign was dominated by his mother's
brother, the Protector Edward Seymour, Duke of Somerset. He showed a rare degree of religious tolerance, a social
conscience against some of the rapacious landowners, and

PARVVLE PATRISSA, PATRIÆ VIRTVTIS ET HÆRES
 ESTO, NIHIL MAIVS MAXIMVS ORBIS HABET.
GNATVM VIX POSSVNT COELVM ET NATVRA DEDISSE,
 HVIVS QVEM PATRIS, VICTVS HONORET HONOS.
ÆQVATO TANTVM, TANTI TV FACTA PARENTIS,
 VOTA HOMINVM, VIX QVO PROGREDIANTVR, HABENT
VINCITO, VICISTI. QVOT REGES PRISCVS ADORAT
 ORBIS, NEC TE QVI VINCERE POSSIT, ERIT.
Ricard.Morysing Car—

sought unsuccessfully the union of England and Scotland. But Somerset was himself greedy and the boy-King disliked his uncle. Somerset was deposed in October 1549 (and eventually executed). The new leader of the government was the Duke of Northumberland, who was ambitious for himself and his family and had none of Somerset's redeeming qualities. Edward VI was the only Tudor to be an enthusiastic Protestant and, some ten months before his death, signed a document prepared by Northumberland which altered the succession so as to exclude his Roman Catholic half-sister, Mary. Edward's nominee was Henry VIII's great-niece, Lady Jane Grey, fifth in line of succession (to whom Northumberland had married his son). On

ABOVE A charming portrait of the infant Edward VI.

RIGHT Edward Seymour, Duke of Somerset, Edward VI's Protector during the early part of his short reign.

Continued on pg 82

THE ELIZABETHAN COURT

When Elizabeth I came to the throne in 1558 it was still assumed that monarchy was a task for strong men rather than allegedly frail women. There had been no female ruler of the first rank for many centuries. Elizabeth had therefore to discover for herself the secret of government. Fortunately she possessed a scholar's mind and a sharp instinct for politics. But allied to these attributes were qualities which defy ready definition and yet enabled her to dominate a masculine world by bewitching it. She was Gloriana, Belphoebe, Diana, the hub of a gallant and glittering Court that owed something to the Italian Renaissance but even more to a pride in insular self-sufficiency discovered only with the Tudors.

At first it was a court mainly of young men, most from families who had only recently attained nobility. Best known among them was Robert Dudley, tall, handsome and a few months older than the Queen herself. Elizabeth appointed him Master of the Horse and he was created Earl of Leicester in 1564. He remained her favourite for thirty years, and she nicknamed him her 'Eyes'. She bestowed pet names on all these leading courtiers. Christopher Hatton, a twenty-four-year-old lawyer, whose dancing in a masque caught the Queen's attention, became her 'Lids'. (Eventually he became her Lord Chancellor, too.) Sir Thomas Heneage, Master of the Twelfth Night revels in 1566 and Vice-Chamberlain, became her 'Sanguine'. Even the wise and sombre Burghley –a Lord Treasurer who constantly protested he was no

courtier–was called her 'Spirit'. It was an agreeably make-believe society of courtly love and allegory.

Yet it was not, as so many other courts were, false and frivolous. It was a principal source for the new literary creativity of the late sixteenth century. A year after the defeat of the Armada, Richard Puttenham compiled a critique of 'English Poesie' in which he commented in detail on ten 'courtly makers of verse who have written excellently well'. Among them were mere generous flatterers like the Earl of Oxford. But two names stand out, Raleigh and Sidney. Sir Walter Raleigh was an adventurer and pioneer colonialist, a man whose doublet was studded with pearls and whose hat carried a black feather fastened with a ruby clasp; but he was also the author of 'the most lofty, insolent and passionate . . . ditties and amorous odes'. Sir Philip Sidney, already dead by 1589, epitomized the ideal of Elizabethan chivalry, a soldier-courtier of courage who could turn an elegantly phrased sonnet.

By 1595 the Court had become a mirror to a passing age. Outwardly the old love-tricks and flirtations, the conceits and artifices of Robert Devereux, Earl of Essex, continued to delight Elizabeth. Even after Essex's disgrace and death, there were still masques, plays and music at court. The new year of 1603 was seen in with all the festivities, which as usual reached a climax on Twelfth Night. But it was the end of the greatest of masques; within three months the Queen was dead, and the Court silent at last.

LEFT Nonsuch, sadly now demolished, was one of the most famous of Tudor palaces.

OPPOSITE Gloriana, carried proudly aloft by her courtiers. Painting attributed to Robert Peake.

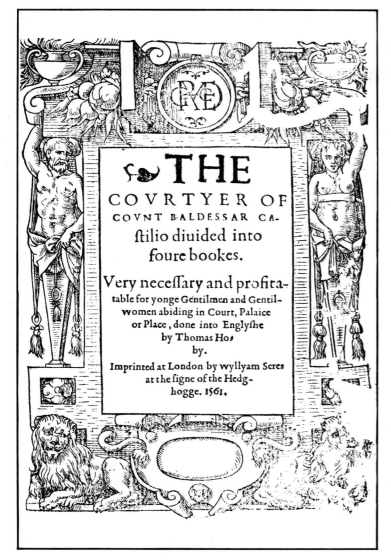

ABOVE William Cecil, Lord Burghley, Elizabeth's great statesman and adviser.

BELOW The Earl of Essex, one of Elizabeth's favourites.

ABOVE Sir Walter Raleigh, adventurer and courtier.

BELOW Robert Dudley, Earl of Leicester, Elizabeth's 'Eyes'.

RIGHT Title page of the English translation of Castiglione's treatise on courtly etiquette.

Sic transit gloria – an allegorical portrait of the aging Elizabeth, with Time and Death.

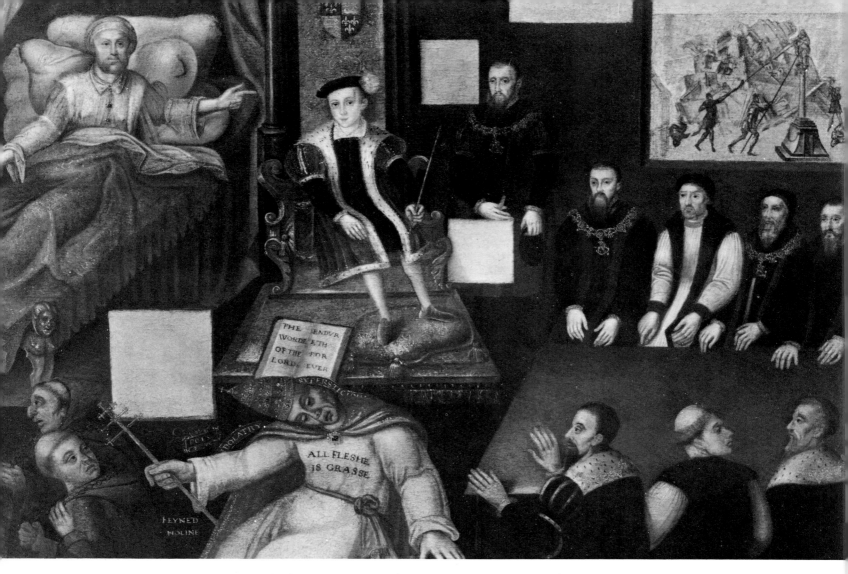

The new King Edward VI, flanked by the dying Henry VIII and Protector Somerset. Only nine years old at his succession, Edward died of tuberculosis six years later.

Edward VI's death Lady Jane was proclaimed Queen in London.

Technically Queen Jane reigned for nine days. The country rejected Northumberland's plot and when Mary Tudor rode into London to claim her throne she was escorted by Elizabeth and by Anne of Cleves, neither of whose sympathies inclined towards Papal doctrines. Mary herself was as strong-willed as any Tudor. She was determined to restore the power of the Church of Rome. Legislation was carried through Parliament providing for a reconciliation, though safeguarding the new owners of the former monastic lands. It was not Mary's Catholicism that alienated her subjects but her marriage to Philip of Spain, whom she wished to be treated as King of England and not merely as her consort. Bitterness at her failure to become pregnant and at the hostility shown in London towards Philip led Mary to revive the laws providing for the burning of heretics. The fires of Smithfield, Oxford and many smaller towns lit, in Bishop Latimer's dying words, 'such a candle, by God's grace, in England as shall never be put out'.

Mary Tudor, saddened by neglect from her husband and by a military debacle which lost England Calais, died in mid-November 1558. The accession of Elizabeth was received by her subjects with a mixture of relief and apprehension. It was assumed she would safeguard narrowly national interests endangered by her half-sister's Spanish proclivities; but no one could predict that a daughter of Anne Boleyn would become the most illustrious of English sovereigns, lauded in her country's literature as her predecessors had never been. Some of this adulation was natural to the fulsome and exaggerated style of the age; some of it became, in due course, respect for longevity, since Elizabeth was the first English ruler to live into her seventieth year; but basically the Queen was hailed as the political genius who mothered the English nation-state through adolescence into maturity. Later generations have emphasized the skill and subtlety of her ministers. William Cecil (Lord Burghley) became her Secretary of State a fortnight after her accession and served her over four decades, and Francis Walsingham was a minister for thirteen critical years. But they were executants of a policy she alone determined. Not least of her gifts was the ability to select wise ministers.

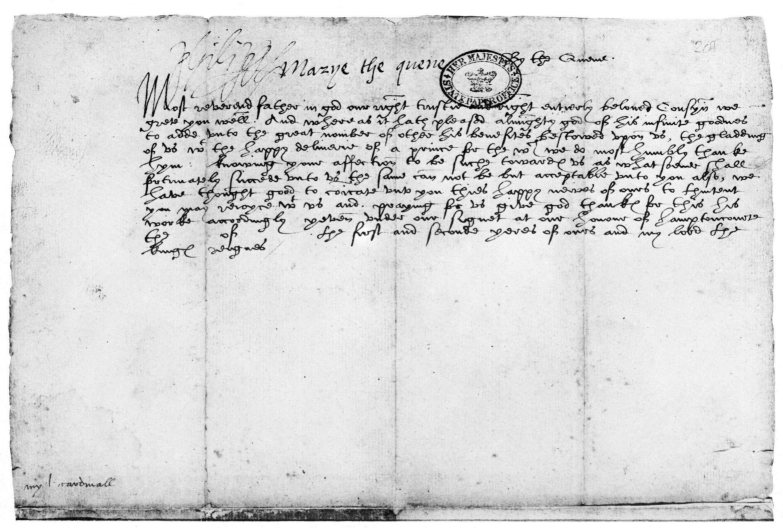

ABOVE Mary Tudor's letter of May 1555 to Cardinal Pole, informing him, mistakenly, that she was pregnant.

Blast and counter-blast in religious propaganda. FAR LEFT 'Exhortation to all menne to take heed and beware of rebellion': a Catholic pamphlet addressed to Queen Mary. LEFT Title page of John Knox's pamphlet of 1558 entitled 'The First Blast of the Trumpet'.

Elizabeth never married. She used spinsterhood as a diplomatic weapon, holding out the prospect of a match in order to gain concessions, notably from France. Her most intense emotional feeling was reserved for Robert Dudley, Earl of Leicester, although in later years she maintained a curious flirtatious masquerade with the dead Leicester's stepson, the Earl of Essex. This relationship, however, ended tragically when Essex entered into a foolish conspiracy and, after an abortive revolt in London, was executed for treason. It is hard to believe Elizabeth possessed physical attraction of a conventional kind. Men admired the range of her intellect, her ready wit, her music and horsemanship. They fell for her judicious flattery and for the use she made of her femininity to arouse their protective instincts, as when she addressed the troops at Tilbury when faced by the threat of invasion in 1588. Often her ministers found her capricious, exacting and exasperating; but they accepted her judgement, her intuitive touch in the craft of kingship.

Her good sense was at its best in the religious settlement of 1559, a compromise retaining the traditional hierarchy in a church which was independent of the Papacy and allowed doctrinal latitude. There was little solely religious persecution. But the danger of a Catholic restoration was considerable. The heir to the throne was Henry VIII's sister's granddaughter, Mary Stuart, Queen of Scots. She was a

The L. Elizabeth Prifoner in the Tower

The L. Elizabeth before her Sifter Q. Mary

Queen Elizabeth rides in Triumph through Lon:

The Spanish Invafion in the Year 1588:

A sequence of scenes in the life of Elizabeth I.

Catholic and could count on foreign aid. From 1586 onwards she was a refugee in the English Midlands, but her presence stimulated a rebellion by the pro-Catholic northern earls in 1569 and subsequently encouraged a series of conspiracies and assassination plots against Elizabeth. In 1586 Mary Stuart was implicated in the notorious Babington conspiracy, and in February 1587 she was executed in Fotheringay Castle, though Elizabeth evaded responsibility for the deed.

The supreme crisis of Elizabeth's reign came in the following year. The English seamen – Drake, Hawkins, Grenville, Raleigh – had long exasperated the Spanish by their expeditions to the Americas and their attempts to secure a share in the Caribbean trade. To such 'piracy' was added, in the eyes of King Philip II, the sin of Elizabeth's heresy. In 1588 he despatched a great fleet of galleons, the Armada, to sail up the Channel and transport a Spanish army of invasion from the Netherlands. But the small English vessels harassed the Armada, disrupting it with fireships and leaving it to be wrecked by storms. Spain's vaunted 'Enterprise of England' proved a fiasco, and Elizabeth basked in the reflected glory of her seamen.

Triumph over the Armada was followed by a sudden release of imaginative creativity. Culturally the last fifteen years of the Elizabethan reign exploded with the genius of Shakespeare, Marlowe, Spenser and Ben Jonson.

6
Stuart Catastrophe 1603~1688

LIZABETH I always disliked discussion of the succession. She seems to have thought that, as with many other matters in her reign, if she waited long enough the problem would solve itself: besides, as she was painfully aware, it was not her business. Certainly the danger of a disputed succession receded after the execution of Mary Stuart and the defeat of the Armada, for a Catholic ruler was now improbable. From 1587 onwards, the rightful claimant was James VI of Scotland, son of Mary Stuart and Lord Darnley, who were themselves both great-grandchildren of Henry VII. In 1602 Elizabeth's Secretary of State, Robert Cecil, began a secret and coded correspondence with James to ensure his peaceful succession. And on 5 April 1603, twelve days after the Queen's death at Richmond, King James VI and I set out from Holyrood on the four-hundred-mile journey south.

He believed it would be easier to govern England than Scotland. 'Saint George', he was heard to remark, 'surely rides upon a towardly riding horse, where I am daily bursting in daunting a wild unruly colt.' James was bitterly conscious of the power exercised by the Scottish Presbyterians: he had twice been kidnapped by his subjects. But he exaggerated the extent of royal supremacy in England, failing to see that what the awe-inspiring Elizabeth had exacted by guile and intimidation, would never be readily offered to a slightly ridiculous Scottish homosexual, excessively fond of his own voice.

James was faced by four main problems: undercover Roman Catholicism; increasing Puritanism; truculence in the House of Commons; and foreign affairs. He was most successful in the last of these matters, securing peace and reconciliation with Spain. Catholic opposition provided the most dramatic episode in the reign, and the thwarting of Guy Fawkes's plot to blow up the opening of Parliament in 1605 is still commemorated each year on 5 November. But, apart from this sensational conspiracy, James was more troubled by the Puritans, especially when they urged replacement of the episcopate by a Presbyterian system of church government. This was too close to his experiences

in Scotland for James's liking: 'No bishop, no king', he complained, after presiding over a conference of Anglican and Puritan churchmen at Hampton Court. Yet he accepted the importance of biblical study to the individual and ordered preparation of an 'Authorised Version' of the Bible in the English of his day. It was published in 1611.

James summoned four Parliaments, 1604–11, 1614, 1621 and 1624–5. Relations between King, lords and commons steadily deteriorated. Elizabeth's later Parliaments had seen MPs claiming special rights of free speech and freedom from arrest, and she had handled them carefully. Under James these claims multiplied, and were linked to protests against the sovereign's grant of commercial monopolies to his favourites and his imposition of new tariffs on merchandise. At the same time the political initiative began to pass from the House of Lords to the Commons. The incipient quarrel between sovereign and Parliament was intensified by the King's manner. For James thought of himself as a learned man. He had published a treatise on the 'True Law of Free Monarchies' five years before coming south: 'Kings are breathing images of God upon earth', he had written. And in London he insisted, time and time again, on lecturing Parliament and his Justices on the supernatural quality of kingship. He was pedantic, dogmatic and intolerant – as in his denunciation of tobacco smoking and his paranoic fantasies about witchcraft – and the parliamentarians responded with political theories of their own. 'The power of the King in Parliament is greater than his power out of Parliament, and doth rule and control it', declared the Member for Great Marlow in the Commons of 1610. Already, thirty years before the Civil War, the sovereign and his people's representatives were striking doctrinaire attitudes poles apart.

Had James been succeeded by a ruler who knew at first hand his subjects and his realm, there was no need for this breach to be perpetuated. But Charles I, who came to the throne in March 1625, knew no one outside his family and his Court. He was the most sheltered king in Europe, a saintly young man of twenty-four, diffident, reserved,

ABOVE Symbolic painting of the succession of Henry VIII. On the left are Mary Tudor and Philip of Spain, with Mars the god of war. On the right is Elizabeth accompanied by Flora and the fruits of prosperity.

LEFT Mary Tudor curing the King's Evil, from a sixteenth-century manuscript.

LEFT Elizabeth I in the garden at Wanstead, a great house now no longer in existence.

ABOVE Sir Christopher Wren in front of his most famous creation, St Paul's Cathedral. The Great Fire of 1666 brought him into prominence as the architect of the new London.

James I, painted by Paul van Somer c. 1620. The King is shown in his state robes in front of the Whitehall Banqueting House then under construction.

excessively formal and aloof. In youth he had accumulated a stock of aphorisms, carefully written out as though in a copy-book. They served as a ready-reckoner substitute for experience: too often they echoed his father, although with James's bawdy pedantry expunged.

That, indeed, was a characteristic of Charles's early years. To Parliament there appeared a disagreeable continuity between the reigns. James I's last favourite, the Duke of Buckingham, retained his influence until his assassination at Portsmouth in August 1628. It was Buckingham who negotiated Charles's marriage to Henrietta Maria of France, the youngest and most vivacious child of the great Henry of Navarre. Unfortunately it was Buckingham,

too, who grafted on to the impressionable Charles his own cavalier pose of impromptu political recklessness, behaviour which ill fitted the solemn introspective nature of the King. Charles's many errors of judgement spring, as much as anything, from this contradiction in character.

Even before Buckingham's murder, Charles was at loggerheads with Parliament over finance and foreign policy. From 1629 to 1640 he tried to rule without Parliament, levying money by reviving antiquated medieval obligations, such as fines for alleged encroachments on the royal forests and further fines on members of the gentry who refused to accept the costly honour of knighthood. Yet most resented of all these burdens was the raising of money for warships by special taxation levied, in 1635 and 1636, on inland counties as well as on seaports (where ship-money was a traditional form of revenue). The rights of the gentry were valiantly championed by John Hampden of Buckinghamshire, who narrowly lost his famous test case against ship money in the law courts during 1637.

Financially, up until 1638, Charles I's experiment in non-parliamentary government was a success, even though it gave every social class in the realm a grievance against the King. But the collection of revenue was only one aspect of this phase of Charles's government. During these eleven years his chief advisers in Church and State were Archbishop Laud and Thomas Wentworth, Earl of Strafford.

Between them they hoped to impose a system of autocratic monarchical government, based upon efficient administration, a policy of 'Thorough', as Laud called it. The Archbishop also favoured a growth of outward ceremonial in religious observance, an attack upon the Puritanism favoured by the parliamentarians. When Laud sought to impose his religious policy upon Scotland, Charles found himself faced with revolt. In order to raise an army, Charles had to increase his revenue; and for this he needed to summon Parliament. From 1640 to 1642 he was on the defensive constitutionally: he had to sacrifice both Strafford and Laud to the revenge of the parliamentarians. But the King refused to admit Parliament's right to deter-

Henrietta Maria with her dwarf,
painted by Van Dyck.

mine structural reforms in the Church of England or to
control the militia, the only armed force in the kingdom
apart from the royal bodyguard. In January 1642 Charles
attempted a royal *coup d'etat*. He entered the House of
Commons seeking to arrest the five leading members of
the opposition but 'the birds had flown'. This reckless
gesture earned the King a magnificently proud rebuke
from Speaker Lenthall, and no sovereign has ever entered
the Commons since that day.

The failure of the King's coup made civil war inevitable.
It began in the following August when Charles raised his
standard at Nottingham. He received support from the
old squirearchy of the north and the west, from the Church,
from the remnants of the feudal aristocracy, and from
Oxford University. Opposed to him were the wealth,
trade and prosperity of London and the east and south. The
King personally fought courageously and with tactical
shrewdness; but in the long run the economic resources of
London told against his cause. The creation by the
parliamentarians of a New Model Army under Oliver
Cromwell, together with support from the Scots, led to
the defeat of the royalists in 1646. But even then Charles
might have survived, since his opponents were quarrelling
among themselves. The King did, indeed, strike a bargain
with the Scots, who invaded England on behalf of a Stuart
sovereign restrained by English rebels. Cromwell and the

ABOVE Engraving by Sebastian Furck of the execution of Charles I in 1649.

army leaders soon gained a rapid victory. To secure their revolution they resolved on placing the King on trial. 'Charles Stuart' was charged with treason in having 'levied war against the Parliament and kingdom of England'.

Charles I, who had at times in his reign seemed weak and vacillating, conducted himself with dignity throughout the last weeks of his life. He refused to acknowledge the legality of his trial and declined to defend his actions. On 30 January 1649 he was beheaded outside the new Stuart palace of Whitehall. On his way to the scaffold Charles passed through his own banqueting hall, with the painted ceiling he had himself commissioned from Rubens – an allegory representing James I enthroned in glory. Bitter irony, and bitter weather! There were ice-floes on the river and a layer of snow in Whitehall. But Charles did not falter. He met death with tragic perfectibility.

A few days later Cromwell's Purged Parliament formally abolished the monarchy: it was 'unnecessary, burdensome and dangerous to the liberty, safety and public interests of the people'. There followed a series of constitutional experiments, each making the status of Oliver Cromwell nearer and nearer to the established royal form, though he declined to take the crown. His Highness the Lord Protector Oliver, soldier and statesman in the mould of the Tudors, did at least merit the honour and awe accorded to him. But there was no reason for the country

OPPOSITE Charles II, a sophisticated man of the world. Painting by Lely, a Dutchman who came to England in 1641, made his name as a fashionable portrait painter, and was knighted by Charles.

Continued on pg 100

LEFT Henry VI attending Parliament.

RIGHT The 1629 Parliament was the last one ever called by Charles I.

LEFT Henry VIII processing to Parliament with his spiritual and temporal peers, 1512.

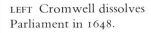

ABOVE Oliver Cromwell, Lord Protector of England.

ABOVE The Great Seal of England, 1651 – the second Seal used in the Commonwealth period.

LEFT Cromwell dissolves Parliament in 1648.

BELOW The House of Commons in 1793, with William Pitt speaking.

Exactly half a century after Magna Carta the first national assembly known as a 'parliament' was summoned to Westminster. The father of 'the mother of parliaments' was the baronial reform leader, Simon de Montfort. Although he died at Evesham later that same year, his experiment survived him. By Edward III's reign the principle of a two-House assembly was well established, and the earliest treatise on parliamentary procedure – the *Modus Tenendi Parliamentum* – may even date from the closing years of Edward II. Edward III summoned, in all, forty-eight Parliaments, and Richard II twenty.

Under the Lancastrian kings Parliament met regularly, but less frequently. Its main task was to grant taxes and consider petitions which would form a basis for legislation. The real advance in power came with the Tudors. Henry VIII facilitated the growth of the Commons by taking the country gentry into partnership with him in government. They became wealthy through the sale of church lands during the Reformation. It was their successors who supported John Pym's revolutionary Grand Remonstrance of November 1641, with its attempt to impose on Charles I the principle of accepting ministers responsible to the Commons. Ultimately the basic issue in the English Civil War was this conflict between King and Parliament.

The Civil War was won by the parliamentarian armies. They did not, however, establish government by the elected representatives of the people. Civil discord was still too great to be resolved by a cumbersome parliament-ary machine. Although Oliver Cromwell experimented with Parliaments elected according to the terms of a written constitution, his administration was essentially a dictatorship. More elected members were excluded from Parliament by the Lord Protector than by any king. Parliament's triumph came with the 'Glorious Revolution' of 1688 and the arrival of William and Mary. For the Declaration of Rights of 1689 denied the sovereign the opportunities to rule by executive decree and guaranteed both freedom of parliamentary election and debate.

Nobody, however, could describe eighteenth-century Britain as a parliamentary democracy. The right to vote varied from district to district. Many constituencies were 'owned' by patrons. Change came gradually in the nineteenth century. The Parliamentary Reform Act of 1832 swept away many anomalies and gave the vote to the landed gentry and the upper-middle classes. The Second Reform Act (1867) allowed most town labourers the vote; and the Third Reform Act (1884) extended the suffrage in the countryside.

The twentieth century has seen the enfranchisement of women and a decline in the powers of the House of Lords. Women over thirty were given the vote in 1918, the age being lowered to twenty-one ten years later. In 1969 the qualifying age for both male and female voters was set at eighteen. Secret ballot dates from 1872. Over the centuries, Parliament has gained in strength by modifying form and function without compromising the values of tradition.

LEFT The House of Lords tries Queen Caroline for immorality in 1820.

BELOW Caricature of William IV as a headmaster expelling the opponents of the Reform Bill, including the Duke of Wellington and Sir Robert Peel, in 1831.

THE HEAD MASTER turning out the INCORRIGIBLES.

Catherine of Braganza, daughter of the King of Portugal, married Charles II in 1662. Miniature by Samuel Palmer.

to respect Richard Cromwell, the amiable but weak son who succeeded to his father's titles in September 1658. A majority of the gentry and the army preferred a restoration; and in the spring of 1660 General Monk and his guards carried through a bloodless coup and proclaimed the succession of Charles II. On 25 May the King arrived at Dover in a warship sent to fetch him from Holland. Four days later he was rapturously received in London. It was his thirtieth birthday.

Samuel Pepys, diarist and Admiralty civil servant, accompanied Charles back to Dover. He records how, on the first evening out, the King 'upon the quarter-deck fell into discourse of his escape from Worcester, where it made me ready to weep to hear the stories he told of his difficulties'. For Charles returned a legendary figure. He had sought his throne abortively in 1651, only to be defeated at the battle of Worcester by Cromwell. For six weeks he was a fugitive, hunted across the Midland shires, down into Dorset and through Hampshire into Sussex, before escaping from 'a creek near Brightelmstone' (Brighton) for Normandy. The romance of the King's adventures, told and retold many times in the years ahead, made Charles a living myth, as no ruler had been since Richard 'the Lion Heart'. But not only was Charles the hero of a great escape story: his wit, manners, tact and commonsense ensured his popularity. Although he had a sense of monarchial dignity, he could even laugh at himself, at least until the last few years of the reign.

But 'old Rowley' was more than 'a merry monarch'; he was as shrewd as any politician of his age. He knew that the triumphant royalist squirearchy wanted to impose a rigid Anglican political establishment, preventing Catholics and dissenters from having any share in government or, indeed, from enjoying the basic civil liberties of a tolerant society. Throughout his reign Charles II tried to hold in check the fanaticism of parliamentarians more royalist than the King. Yet, in a modified form he faced the problem his father and grandfather had known. He needed a sound and regular revenue in order to maintain an effective army and navy; but the political leaders hesitated to allow Charles the money, in case it made the crown independent of parliamentary restraint. Hence in 1670 Charles was forced to turn to Louis XIV of France, from whom he received funds in secret, holding out to Louis the prospect of improving the status of the Roman Catholics in England and of joining the French in their war against the Dutch. Only a man with Charles's good political instinct could have maintained such a devious policy for so long. It is questionable whether alliance with the French monarchy, the strongest military power in Europe, was in England's best interests, although the Dutch were the chief colonial and maritime rivals of the City of London.

ABOVE Nell Gwynne with her two sons by Charles II – Charles, Duke of St Albans, and James, Lord Beauclerk. Engraving after Gascar.

LEFT The first page of the Act of Attainder against the Duke of Monmouth. Charles II's favourite illegitimate son, who had landed in the West Country and organized a Protestant rebellion.

Anno Regni

Jacobi II. Regis.

An Act to Attaint *James* Duke of *Monmouth* of High-Treaſon.

 Whereas James Duke of Monmouth has in an Hoſtile manner In= vaded this Kingdom, and is now in open Rebellion, Levying War againſt the King, contrary to the Duty of his Al- legiance; Be it Enacted by the Kings

B 2   most

Allegorical print depicting the flight of James II to France and the arrival of William and Mary from the Netherlands in 1688.

The political record of Restoration England is, however, unedifying. By contrast, and as if to compensate for Cromwellian austerity, music and the arts flourished under royal patronage. The theatre too was free from puritanical censorship. Yet if it was the age of Dryden, Wycherley, Purcell and Kneller, it was also an age of science. In July 1662 Charles II founded the Royal Society, the first scientific institution established with monarchical patronage anywhere in Europe. The King himself was no more than a dilettante scientist, yet he could hold his own in conversation with the great names of the institution – the physicist Boyle, the inventor Hooke, later the astronomer Halley and, above all, the mathematician and physicist Isaac Newton. Charles, however, never intended to limit the Royal Society to the narrowly scientific aspects of knowledge. He knew no barrier between a scientific and a non-scientific culture. Among the founder Fellows of the Royal Society were the poets Dryden and Waller, the diarist Evelyn, and the antiquarian Aubrey.

The founder Fellow who made the greatest contribution to the outward form of Restoration England was the architect Christopher Wren. On 3 September 1666 Charles II personally took control in the City of London commanding workmen and fire-fighters struggling to check the flames which threatened to engulf his capital. When the Great Fire was contained, it was the King who urged Wren to prepare plans for a new city. Although Wren's designs proved too expensive and ambitious to be implemented in full, Charles at the council table saved enough of Wren's ideal to ensure that the new London was nobler and more spacious than the mass of narrow streets through which plague had swept in one year and fire in the next.

But the Great Fire had started the most terrible rumours. It was said, without a shred of evidence, to have been the work of papists; and for the last nineteen years of Charles II's reign he had to combat the ugly anti-Catholic mood of the Londoners and of Parliament. It prevented any advance in religious toleration and in 1678 assumed the proportions of a mass hysteria when the demagogue Titus Oates revealed an alleged Popish Plot, a Jesuit conspiracy to murder Charles and place his Roman Catholic brother, the Duke of York, on the throne. The frenzy reached ridiculous lengths. The liveliest of Charles's mistresses, Nell Gwynne, found herself hemmed in by a mob which had mistaken her for one of her 'Papist' rivals: 'Good people, I am the *Protestant* whore', she was forced to declare before being allowed to pass into the royal palace. Charles himself never believed in the plot. He was relieved when Oates was eventually discredited. But in two years his perjuries had led, directly or indirectly, to more than thirty judicial murders. And throughout the last six years of his reign Charles had to fend off parliamentary demands to exclude his brother from the succession. For, though Charles fathered eight illegitimate sons by five mistresses, his marriage to Catherine of Braganza remained childless; and the Duke of York, three years his junior in age, was rightful heir to the throne.

Charles died in February 1685, accepting Catholic rites in the last hour of his life. Despite the attempts at exclusion the Duke of York was proclaimed King James II. The reign began peacefully enough. Parliament voted him generous funds but annoyed him by seeking to publish a proclamation enforcing laws against all dissenters from the Church of England. The King intended to secure civil equality for Catholics and Nonconformists alike. The old Catholic nobility of England urged him to show sense and moderation, but these were qualities he had never possessed. When the Duke of Monmouth, Charles II's favourite illegitimate son, landed in the West Country and encouraged a Protestant revolt, public opinion supported the King. But the cruelty of Judge Jeffrey's Assize, which followed the suppression of Monmouth's rising, alienated the moderates. James II raised and maintained a standing army which he hoped would overawe London; he prosecuted seven Anglican bishops, violated the rights of both the ancient universities, and placed Roman Catholics in key military positions.

The Protestants consoled themselves with the thought that the heir presumptive was not Catholic. If James died, the throne would pass to Mary, his elder daughter by his first wife, Anne Hyde. Mary had married her cousin, William of Orange, leader of the Dutch in their struggle against Louis XIV of France. William, the son of Charles II's sister, was strongest male claimant to the English throne.

But in June 1688 James II's wife, Mary of Modena, gave birth to a son – later known as the 'Old Pretender'. This threat of a permanent Catholic dynasty induced six politicians and Bishop Compton of London secretly to invite William to claim the throne on behalf of his wife, alleging the baby's birth was an imposture. That autumn the English waited, with mixed feelings, for a 'Protestant wind' which would bring a Dutchman to save their traditional liberties. The wind carried William of Orange west of Brixham, where he landed on 5 November. As he advanced on London, James's support melted away. The King sought to flee across the Channel but was ignominiously brought back to Whitehall before being sent on his travels again by his Dutch nephew. James landed at Ambleteuse on Christmas Day and lived on in France, mostly at St Germain, for another dozen years.

7
Protestant Establishment 1688~1820

T HE flight of James II left the throne technically vacant, and it was at first not clear precisely how it was to be filled. Effective power was in the hands of William of Orange although his consort Mary (who, after James II's infant son, was rightful heir) remained in Holland. William summoned a Convention 'Parliament' which met on 1 February 1689. In three weeks it agreed on the principles of a revolutionary constitutional settlement. These were embodied in a Declaration of Rights which denounced the 'illegalities' of the previous reign, notably the maintenance of a peacetime standing army and the King's claim to dispense with the laws. There was at first a suggestion that William should be regent and Mary Queen; but they insisted on a joint tenure of the throne and, after Mary had come over to join her husband in February, they were proclaimed as King William III and Queen Mary II.

In effect the Convention ensured that henceforth the possession of the crown depended upon parliamentary consent. Subsequent acts during William and Mary's reign confirmed the supremacy of parliament. The Triennial Act of 1694 required a new Parliament to be summoned every three years; Mutiny Acts, normally valid for only twelve months at a time, gave the Commons control over the raising of an army; parliamentary approval was required for the dismissal of judges and for royal expenditure in an annual 'Civil List': and finally, in 1701, an Act of Settlement required future monarchs to be members of the Church of England, and not to leave the kingdom without parliamentary sanction. A religious settlement was also reached which guaranteed Protestant Nonconformists freedom of worship, under certain safeguards (Toleration Act, 1689); but technically Nonconformists remained excluded from public affairs.

William III was frequently irritated by party politics. He had one ambition in life; the toppling of Louis XIV of France from his mastery of Europe. Mary was occasionally haunted by guilt at having deposed her father. But William had no qualms. If his father-in-law supported Louis, he

had to be defeated: first, in England in 1688; two years later, at the battle of the Boyne when James tried to establish a foothold in Ireland. Londonderry might revere William of Orange as a Protestant deliverer, but he was no religious fanatic – he was the enemy of France. Everything was subordinate to the war. Even the establishment of the Bank of England in 1694 was intended to make it easier for the government to raise immediate money to keep an army in the field and the fleet at sea. When Mary died from smallpox in 1695, William, although wretched at heart from his loss, continued to reign on his own, with a patriotic association rallying to protect him when it was learnt that agents from France were planning his assassination. There was, at times, a feeling in London that he thought more of his Dutch inheritance than of his kingdom. In the last five years of his reign he was especially criticized for his tortuous diplomacy: the treaty of Ryswick of 1697 had curbed French power and secured formal recognition of Louis XIV of the dynastic settlement of 1688; but by 1701 William was convinced that war would be resumed and he began to build up a new European coalition.

By now, however, William was worn-out, suffering badly from dropsy. On 20 February 1702 he was thrown from his horse, which had stumbled on a mole-hill in the parkland of Hampton Court, the Tudor palace to which William and Mary had given a new Dutch appearance. He never fully recovered from his fall, dying at Kensington on 8 March 1702.

William was succeeded by James II's surviving daughter, Anne, who in the first speech after her accession emphasized that her 'own heart' was 'entirely English'. She was a pathetic figure – only thirty-seven when she came to the throne, but physically weakened by seventeen pregnancies. Inevitably to many at Court she appeared plain, gouty, dumpy and dim. Less than two years previously she suffered the bitterness of losing the only one of her children to survive infancy. William, Duke of Gloucester, a highly intelligent boy, contracted a fatal fever immediately after his eleventh birthday celebrations. All these misfortunes

THE
Proteſtant Triumph:
OR,
The ſignal Victory of K. *William* over the *French* and *Iriſh*,

Chaſing them from Hill to Hill, taking their Arms and Ammunition alſo ; the
Surrender of *Drogheda*, and the King's entring the City of *Dublin* ; to the un-
ſpeakable Joy and Satisfaction of all True Proteſtants.

This Victory was obtain'd on Tueſday the Firſt of *July* 1690.

To the Tune of The Spinning wheel.   Licenſed according to Order.

DUBLIN.

BRave Boys, let Bells now ſweetly ring,
and flowing Bowls go freely roun,
with Hearts to our moſt gracious King,
who is this day with Triumph Crown'd:
A Fig for all our Romiſh Foes,
K. William Conquers where he goes.

While Trumpets ſounded Victory,
and rattling Warlike Drums did beat;
We laugh'd to ſee the Tories flee,
in total Confuſion they retreat,
While we purſu'd with hardy Blows,
K. William Conquers where he goes.

The French and Torys hearts did ake,
as ſoon as e'er we drew to near,
And did their Poſts ſoon forſake,
being glad to run away for fear :
They knew they could not us oppoſe,
K. William Conquers where he goes.

To Ardee Paſs we march'd with ſpeed,
where many Thouſand Tories lay,
Who being the right Iriſh Breed,
they took to heels and run away :
K. William he ſuch Courage ſhows,
Which Conquers where e'er he goes.

Our right renowned King reply'd,
March on, my valiant warlike Boys,
For we ſhall ſoon ſubdue the Pride
of both the French and the Dear-joys :
Thus did he Chaſe his flying Foes,
and Conquers all where e'er he goes.

King William Marching in the Head,
while Trumpets did moſt ſweetly ſound,
And all our flying Colours ſpread,
which fight did all our Foes renfound :
K. William's Courage ſcares his Foes,
He Conquers all where e'er he goes.

At length we had a bloudy Fray,
our Guns like Thunder then did roar,
K. William he did win the day,
and laid the French in reeking Gore :
His Courage ſcares his mighty Foes,
He conquers all where e'er he goes.

Now while the Fight we did maintain,
we made the Torp Rebells run ;
Lord Carlingford be being ſlain,
and many Great Commanders too :
K. William's Courage daunts his Foes,
He Conquers all where e'er he goes.

Stout Colonel Parker, with his Teagues,
likewiſe lay bleeding on the Ground,
We ſcourg'd them for their late Intriegues,
while our King is with Trophies Crown'd :
To Dublin Gates he chas'd his Foes,
He Conquers all where e'er he goes.

The King he ſent to Drogheda,
to yield before it was too late ;
Or elſe his roaring Guns he'd play,
with that they did ſurrender ſtraight ;
Now they could not him oppoſe,
Who Conquers all where e'er he goes.

Late James he quitted Dublin ſtraight,
And great King William did march in,
'Tis joyful Tydings to relate,
how he do's Fame and Honour win :
His Courage ſcares the mighty Foes,
He Conquers, &c.

Our Proteſtants he did free,
which in cloſe Priſons long hath lain,
They all enjoy their Liberty,
under K. William who do's Reign
In ſpight of all inſulting Foes ,
He Conquers all where e'er he goes.

Printed for P. Brooksby, J. Deacon, J. Blare, J. Back.

LEFT Broadsheet celebrating
William of Orange's victory
over the French and Irish at the
battle of the Boyne, and his
triumphant entry into Dublin.

BELOW Political cartoon of
1690, entitled 'The Protestant
Grindstone'. William and Mary
look on while the Archbishop
of Canterbury and the Bishop
of London grind the Pope's
nose.

Queen   *King*   *Schomberg*

Old Holy Father, there was once a time
When Clemency was thought a mortall Crime
For Hereticks no pitty you could find :
But most severely did their Faces Grind.

The time's now turn'd, harsh Stripes upon you fall.
Too well deserv'd, and this is done that all
Who see the Whore of Babylon may Say,
Shee's vex't because her nose is worn away.

intensified religious conviction; she conscientiously ful-filled her responsibilities as a sovereign and as head of the Church. From her royal resources she established a 'bounty', to augment the value of the poorer Anglican clergy's earnings. She was devoted to her husband, Prince George of Denmark, a dull and dutiful nonentity who dabbled in mathematics. Personally Anne liked to play cards, admire old English gardens, and drink tea which was sometimes fortified with gin.

Most of all Anne enjoyed the company of Sarah Churchill, her friend since childhood. Sarah – vivacious, scheming and imperious – was five years Anne's senior in years, and never forgot it. Their unusual relationship, in which the Queen would call Sarah 'Mrs Freeman' and expected to be called 'Mrs Morley' in reply, had political consequences. It ensured the primacy within the army of Sarah's husband, John, who was created Duke of Marlborough in 1702 and was acknowledged as the supreme strategic genius of his age. Linked in Anne's mind with John and Sarah Churchill was their friend Sydney Godolphin, whom the Queen made Lord Treasurer on her accession (and to whom contemporaries sometimes referred as 'the prime minister', a title never used before).

The kingdom was at war with France for almost all of

Glorification of Queen Anne, celebrating the victories of the Allies up to the battle of Vigo Bay, 1702. William III watches over her, while Honour kills Deceit and Envy.

ABOVE LEFT James II, painted by Lely.

ABOVE RIGHT James II's first wife, Anne Hyde, painted by Lely.

LEFT Mary of Modena, James II's second wife, painted by Kneller.

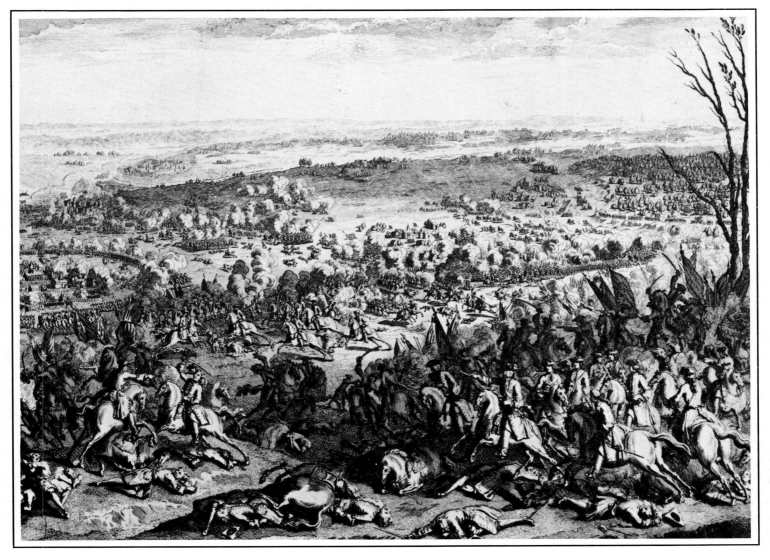

OPPOSITE The apotheosis of William and Mary, from Thornhill's superb painted ceiling in the Royal Naval College at Greenwich, formerly the Royal Hospital.

Marlborough's resounding victory at the battle of Blenheim in 1704 shattered the myth of French invincibility in the field. The French King Louis XIV was so horrified that he forbade all mention of the battle.

Anne's reign. 'Marlborough's wars' differed from the campaigns of William III: they covered a wider area and they consciously related military and naval operations. In 1704 the Duke led a composite English, Dutch and German army deep into Europe in pursuit of the French, who were threatening Vienna, the capital of his chief ally. The Duke's victory on the upper Danube at Blenheim on 13 August 1704 saved Austria and allowed the British to celebrate their greatest success on land since Agincourt. It was followed by Ramillies (1706), Oudenarde (1708) and Malplaquet (1709), battles won in present-day Belgium, where Marlborough established a barrier against the French. These were years of triumph. They saw, as well, the acquisition of Gibraltar and of important territories flanking the French possessions in Canada. In 1707 Godolphin's ministry carried through an Act of Union, linking at last the English and Scottish Parliaments and the economy both sides of the border (a measure thought in London to favour the Scots). But by 1709 the country was tiring of the Whig magnates who favoured a continental war; their political enemies, the Tories, began to accuse Marlborough of wasting English and Scottish blood; and there was a hope of peace.

'We four must never part until death mows us down with his impartial hand', Anne had written to Duchess Sarah in the summer of 1703, when the partnership of the Marlboroughs and Godolphin was beginning. The Queen, enjoying the reflected glory of the Duke's victories, allowed the Marlboroughs to bask in her favour. Vanbrugh's Blenheim Palace, the largest private house in England, sprang up at Woodstock, where the medieval kings held court; it was a gift to a great soldier from his sovereign. But in 1708–9 a rift developed between the Queen and Sarah, partly over Anne's friendship with a lady in waiting, Abigail Masham. Sarah was a Whig,

Continued on pg 113

THE INDUSTRIAL REVOLUTION

During the sixty-year reign of George III the appearance of the English landscape changed dramatically. Although there had been enclosures in some regions for a couple of centuries, in 1760 the countryside was still predominantly open, with wild heath, thickets and woodland. Towns were trading centres first and foremost: if they possessed industries at all, this was a matter for note and comment by surprised travellers. By 1820 it was different. The countryside had taken on the familiar chessboard appearance of carefully hedged acres. In Yorkshire, Lancashire and the Midland counties the skyline was broken by sulphurous chimneys, pit-shafts, and gaunt mills with grim, grey-slated dwellings squatting among them and spreading outwards every year. This was the social reality behind the process which in 1880 was named the 'Industrial Revolution'.

It was a revolution without a precise beginning. For many years experiments had sought increased production by substituting mechanical power for the work of humans and animals. The earliest power-driven factory in England opened at Derby in 1719, using water from the river Soar to 'throw' (i.e. spin) silk. Soon textile mills were going up beside other streams and the traditional cottage industries within the villages faced the challenge of large-scale competition. The textile industry was transformed between 1764 and 1779 by the genius of three Lancastrians: James Hargreaves who invented the spinning jenny, Richard Arkwright the water frame, and Samuel Crompton who combined these two inventions in his spinning mule. Yet the greatest of these early technologists was James Watt who, by patenting a condenser in 1765, was able nine years later to construct a steam engine. The decisive episode in applied science came in 1785 when, for the first time, a steam engine with a rotary movement rather than with the up-and-down movement associated with pumping was installed by Watt (and Matthew Boulton) in a Nottinghamshire cotton-spinning factory. Steam-turned wheels were the dominant feature of the Industrial Revolution.

Watt's inventions came at a time when the traditional timber stocks of England were running low. The steam engine made use of the rich coal deposits of the north and the Midlands. In many cases iron was close at hand, and soon iron-smelting processes were converting the western Midlands into the 'Black Country'. The social and political consequences of these changes in industrial life were enormous. There was an internal migration of peoples from south to north. British commercial prosperity, so long dependent on London and its trade, had found a different centre of gravity.

Yet the Industrial Revolution could never have become so widespread without improved communications. Canal builders provided England with a slow but effective network of waterways. Turnpike roads linked new manufacturing towns to old ports. After 1814 the 'macadamized' road surface allowed stage coaches to bowl along at faster and faster speeds: the 'Royal Telegraph' Day Coach boasted of travelling from London to Manchester in eighteen hours. But, once again, it was steam power that determined the future. Stephenson's 'Rocket' of October 1829 signalled the triumph of industrial invention: first Great Britain, and soon the world, entered the Railway Age.

ABOVE Canals provided cheap and convenient transport for factories in the industrial north. LEFT Opie's allegorical painting of the industrial landowner and the miner, with Watt's engine in the background.

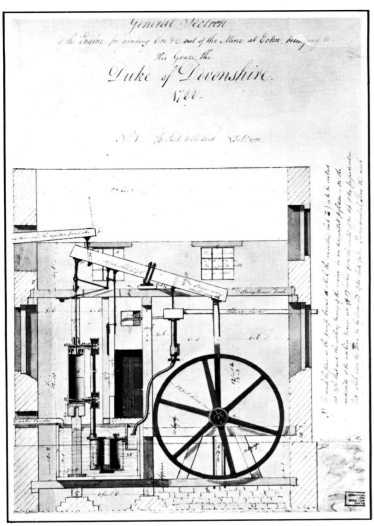

ABOVE Water and steam power in Shropshire – an iron foundry, a boring mill and, on the right, a water wheel.

BELOW Iron aqueduct designed by Robert Fulton, one of the great inventive geniuses of the eighteenth century.

ABOVE James Watt's original working drawing, dated 1788, for 'winding Ore &C out of the Mine at Ecton'.

BELOW Contemporary engraving of Newcomen's steam-pump used in English mines in the eighteenth century.

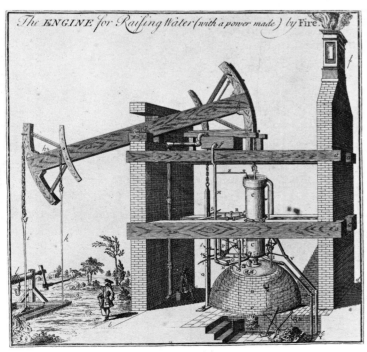

BELOW A Yorkshire collier. Aquatint by R. D. Havell after a drawing by G. Walker, 1813

ABOVE Rural England contrasts sharply with this masterpiece of Victorian engineering.

ABOVE Cartoon of the Earl of Oxford as puppet-master, stage-managing the accession of George I.

Abigail a Tory; and as the Queen began to find Abigail temperamentally less demanding than Sarah, so she inclined more and more to the moderate Tories. They were, after all, like herself pillars of Anglican orthodoxy.

In 1711 Godolphin fell and a Tory ministry won a General Election. As soon as possible the Tories ousted Marlborough and secured peace at Utrecht in 1713. The settlement confirmed most of the early British gains and checked French ambitions. Yet when, a year later, Anne's health began to deteriorate, the Tories fell apart. One faction, ignoring Tory dependence on Anglican sentiment, secretly negotiated with the Jacobite supporters of James II's exiled son, the Roman Catholic 'Old Pretender'. But the Act of Settlement had promised the throne to the Dowager Duchess Sophia of Hanover, granddaughter of James I, and her heirs provided they were Protestants. Sophia died early in 1714, to be followed on the first day of August by Queen Anne herself. The throne therefore passed to Sophia's son George, Elector of Hanover. The Tories were discredited by their Jacobite wing, and it was the Whigs who were to flourish under early Hanoverian rule, although parties were so little unified that there were always dissident Whig groups prepared to oppose and unseat their leaders.

Many years previously George I had sought Anne's hand in marriage, but the Court of Charles II had found him a bore and a boor. Now he was fifty-four, set in his ways and no more attractive. For the past twenty years his wife had been virtually imprisoned, for she had behaved indiscreetly with a dashing Swedish officer, Count Königsmark. George I brought to London, not his consort, but two elderly German mistresses: one was tall and ugly, and nicknamed by the Londoners 'the Maypole'; the other was fat and uglier, and was known as 'the Elephant and Castle'. The King had little idea of the dignity of monarchy and even less of how the compromise constitutional settlement of 1688–9 really functioned. He hardly spoke English at all and an inner council of ministers began to meet which would decide policy under the chairmanship of the leading politician, not the sovereign. By 1720 this new style of 'cabinet government' had thrown up a master manager of the House of Commons, Robert Walpole. That year a major financial concern, the South Sea Company, collapsed and there was a clamour against many figures in politics and at Court who seemed guilty of fraud. But Walpole's coolheadedness prevented outbursts against the Hanoverian dynasty.

Walpole became indispensable to the crown. George I did not like him, and Walpole himself despised everything Hanoverian. It made no difference. He headed a government continuously from 1721 until the beginning of 1742. So successfully did he monopolize power and encourage

OPPOSITE George I and his family, from the Painted Hall at the Royal Naval College, Greenwich.

BUBBLE CARD.

The Headlong Fools Plunge into South Sea Water,
But the Sly Long-heads Wade with Caution a'ter,
The First are Drowning but the Wiser Last,
Venture no Deeper than the Knees or Wast.
1720.

LEFT A contemporary print satirizing the 'headlong fools' who invested everything in the South Sea Company and lost the gamble.

OPPOSITE George II – the last British monarch to lead his troops in battle – on the field at Dettingen.

the growth of collective responsibility within a cabinet that he is generally regarded as the first real Prime Minister.

In June 1727 George I suffered a stroke while visiting Hanover and died in the same room at Osnabrück in which he had been born. His successor, George II, was better-looking and more cultured than his father, with whom he had been on bad personal terms for many years. The new Queen, Caroline of Anspach, was an amply proportioned German blonde, highly intelligent though with a flirtatious bawdiness well-suited to the London society of her day. It was Caroline, rather than her husband, who retained the Walpole ministry, if only because the Prime Minister's worldly cynicism corresponded so closely with her own. Walpole's determination to keep Britain at peace strengthened the national economy and helped to develop trade.

With Caroline's death in 1737 Walpole's tenure of office

seemed less assured. George II, who had fought at Oudenarde, believed in settling vexatious disputes by war. A conflict with Spain sprang up in 1739 over trading rights. The French were allies of Spain and soon all the old animosity between France and England had come once more to the surface. Walpole, who lacked the patriotic zeal of a war leader, resigned in February 1742.

The bungled military operations of the following six years brought no credit to any politician. But in June 1743 George II's personal stock rose. He gained a victory over the French at Dettingen, the last occasion a British king led his army into battle under fire. Perhaps it was partly this increase in royal prestige that turned the Jacobite threat of 1745 into a fiasco. Outwardly the Jacobites should have had in Charles Edward, the grandson of James II, a romantic leader far more attractive than any stolid Hanoverian widower. But though the 'Young Pretender' gained a

following in Scotland, the English remained unresponsive once the 'Forty-five' crossed the border. The Jacobites reached Derby, one hundred and thirty miles from London, but turned back when they found no prominent English figures were shifting their loyalty. The Hanoverian succession was made secure by the ruthless repressive policy imposed on Highland Scotland by George II's favourite son, the Duke of Cumberland. In reality, the 'Old Pretender', who had reached Preston in 1715, had been a more serious threat to the monarchy, although his efforts were never so well co-ordinated as the southward march of his son.

It was easier for Cumberland to stamp out Jacobitism than for the Whigs to fight a victorious war against France without a clear strategic plan. In 1748 Europe was outwardly pacified by the treaty of Aix-la-Chapelle, a settlement which was really no better than a truce. When war

was renewed between Britain and France in May 1756, the British once again fared badly at first. By the end of the year George II had no alternative to appointing as Prime Minister the insufferably proud William Pitt. 'I know that I can save my country and that no one else can', he boasted; and he was right. There was a long cavalcade of victory, extending into the final year of George II's reign. While the French might hold their continental supremacy in Europe, they were losing an empire to the British in North America and India, and mastery of the seas passed to the Royal Navy. Clive, in 1757, had begun the triumphs by defeating the Francophile Siraj-ud-Daula's army at Plessey and then had driven the French traders out of Bengal. A year later two key French settlements in America, Louisburg and Fort Duquesne (now Pittsburg)) fell to the English; and in 1759 the French lost Guadeloupe and, above all, the citadel of Quebec. Pitt gave George II a concept of

ABOVE The Royal Firework Display – immortalized by Handel's music – celebrated the treaty of Aix-la-Chapelle in 1748.

OPPOSITE George III, Queen Charlotte and their large family, painted by Zoffany.

grand strategy unknown in his earlier wars.

George II did not live to celebrate final victory. He died suddenly in October 1760 and was succeeded by his twenty-two-year-old grandson, George III. The new King, like Anne, prided himself on his Britishness (and indeed he never once left his homeland). He was a man of strong partialities and impeccable morals, religious, conscientious, hard-working, and filled with a sense of mission. His two predecessors, with their German background and deep concern for Hanover, had allowed the initiative in government to pass out of royal hands. George III, on the other hand, was educated to rule. He ascended the throne conscious of his vocation but humiliatingly aware of his inadequacies. Within a few years politicians and pamphleteers, puzzled by his confused attempts to fulfil the duties of kingship as he understood them to be, were accusing George of some ambitious scheme of reviving the near-despotism of the Stuarts, though with a Protestant basis of power. His failure was emphasized by the disruption of his empire in the Americas and by radical violence in the reform movements at home. For long he was a butt for historians, many of whom were writing with a Whig-Liberal distrust of royal authority, whether real or imaginary. In consequence, George III is the most maligned of all British monarchs.

At his accession, George III hoped to clean up London society and free his kingdom from governmental corruption. His letters regret he was forced to live in 'a degenerate age . . . in which every virtue is absorbed into vice and dissipation'. He seems to have believed the kingdom could be purged by the work of his old tutor, Lord Bute, whom he made Prime Minister – and then found he had to indulge in corruption himself in order to ensure that Bute had any power in the House of Commons. By 1770, with Bute discredited and the Earl of Chatham (as Pitt had become) broken in health, George looked elsewhere for a Prime Minister in whom he could have confidence and thought he had found one in Lord North. For over ten tumultuous years North retained the King's favour and his majority in Parliament. Probably, under normal conditions, North would have been a good second-class head of a government. But the times were far from normal. His ineptitude in imposing coercion on the American colonies rather than in seeking a compromise which would have allowed the Americans control of their own economic interests ensured for Lord North a permanent low rating among Britain's Prime Ministers. When North resigned in March 1782 his policies had cost George an army and thirteen colonies.

George himself recovered his esteem. In December 1783 he selected Chatham's son, William Pitt, to form a government. It seemed ridiculous to choose a man of twenty-four

Pub.d Nov. 25. 1788. by I. W. Fores N.o 3 Piccadilly.

at such a time, but Pitt stayed in office as long as Walpole earlier in the century. Like Walpole he restored Britain's trade and prosperity. George III, however, did not long enjoy peace of mind. In November 1788 he became seriously ill. Nowadays it is believed he was suffering from a disease of the blood known as porphyria, which affects the nervous system; but porphyria was only identified between the world wars and in 1788 it was assumed 'the royal malady' was a form of madness. Yet by the following summer George seemed fit again. Unfortunately it was the summer of the great French Revolution which cast a shadow over the King's remaining years.

In 1793 Britain went to war to check the spread of revolution from France into Belgium. Pitt, like his father, proved an admirable war leader, and George loyally supported him. But the King remained staunchly Protestant. In 1801 he opposed Pitt's proposals for 'Catholic Emancipation', a measure promising civil rights to George's Roman Catholic subjects, and so Pitt resigned. The menace of Napoleonic invasion brought him back to power, and the King himself prepared to meet the challenge. It did not come. Nelson's triumph at Trafalgar in October 1805 finally removed the threat and ensured

ABOVE A cartoon, cynically entitled 'Filial Piety', on the Regency Crisis of 1788.

British mastery of the seas.

Three months after Trafalgar, Pitt died, exhausted by the war. George III helped form a coalition 'Ministry of All the Talents' to ensure that the struggle was continued. But he, too, succumbed to the strain. In 1810 his mind became totally clouded. This time there was no hope of recovery; and on 5 February 1811 his eldest son assumed the royal prerogative as Prince Regent. George III, unaware of the world around him, lived on at Windsor Castle, where he died in January 1820.

OPPOSITE George III as the mad and senile recluse of Windsor.

8
Expansion and Prosperity 1820~1901

GEORGE III's eldest son became Prince Regent in February 1811 and succeeded to the throne, as George IV, in January 1820. Like his father, the Prince Regent has been roughly handled by historians, although for different reasons. The domestic life of George III and Queen Charlotte of Mecklenburg-Strelitz was always above reproach and it was the King's conscientious attempt to assert the authority of the crown which aroused criticism. But his successor was blamed for his indolence, his love of pleasure, his moral laxity and – though more obliquely – for having, as Regent and King, neglected the Whig politicians who had supported him as a young man. Certainly throughout his life nature inclined George IV to expansive gestures of extravagance. Even before coming of age he was heavily in debt, and debates on the financial problems of the heir to the throne enlivened the House of Commons from 1787 onwards. It was easy for journalists, pamphleteers and cartoonists to ridicule this floridly handsome young man of good taste, with his mania for building and the decorative arts. Yet his money was not all casually thrown away. He prided himself on being a connoisseur of elegant living, and the artistic treasures he accumulated have contributed richly to the cultural heritage of the nation. His patronage of the architect, John Nash, gave London a planned system of crescents, squares and open places, and Brighton the Royal Pavilion.

In 1784 George, then aged twenty-two, fell in love with Maria Fitzherbert, a Roman Catholic widow six years his senior in age. They were secretly married at the end of the following year, but since the ceremony was not sanctioned by the King, it was contrary to the Royal Marriage Act of 1772 and therefore not valid under English law. In 1795 George was married to his cousin, Caroline of Brunswick. Although a daughter, Princess Charlotte, was born a year later, George and Caroline loathed one another. From 1796 onwards they lived apart. George's alleged philanderings at Brighton and his uncertain relationship with Marie Fitzherbert were savagely exposed in the press, which always tended to sympathize with Caroline even though her own behaviour was blatantly amoral. Soon after the accession of George IV, Caroline – who had, for several years, been living in Italy – returned to London and sought recognition of her rights as Queen Consort. George's unsuccessful attempt to have a Bill passed through Parliament which would have annulled his marriage to Caroline because of her scandalous conduct added to his unpopularity in London. The mob that hooted at the King knew nothing of his kindness of heart; his delight in holding children's parties; his eagerness to reprieve prisoners condemned to execution.

The sad record of George IV's marital and extra-marital affairs have tended to distract from his achievements as King. His state visits to Dublin and Edinburgh were highly successful, and helped to reconcile outlying regions of the United Kingdom to a dynasty which had seemed to neglect them. As patron of the arts he encouraged the growth of what was to become the National Gallery and the British Museum. Moreover, though his ministers regarded him as politically untrustworthy in domestic politics, he had a sound understanding of European diplomacy and his judgement was respected by continental statesmen. If occasionally in his last years he gave the impression that he had fought at Waterloo, this fantasy sprang from the bitterness of his heart. Throughout the Napoleonic Wars he had vainly begged his father for a military command in the field. He was nominal Colonel-in-Chief of the Tenth Hussars, with whom he had been in camp and on exercises. At Waterloo it was the Tenth Hussars who broke through the French line and bore down upon Napoleon's vaunted Old Guard. When, five years later, George IV was shown around the battlefield by the Duke of Wellington, it is small wonder if he came emotionally to identify himself with his brother officers, whom he had known so well. He was not mad, nor strictly speaking was he a liar; he remained the most intelligent and imaginative member of the House of Hanover, a Walter Mitty character among the Kings of England.

The Prince Regent – later
George IV – painted as a
dashing young gallant by the
studio of Lawrence.

A BRIGHTON BREAKFAST or *Morning Comforts*

ABOVE The Regency period excelled in the *genre* of the crude and vulgar cartoon – this one satirizes the Prince Regent's relationship with Mrs Fitzherbert.

LEFT Tasteless or magnificent, depending on one's feelings, Nash's Brighton Pavilion reflects the oriental influence in early nineteenth-century architecture and decor.

122

His only child, Princess Charlotte, died tragically in giving birth to a stillborn son in November 1817, eighteen months after her marriage to Prince Leopold of Saxe-Coburg. The tragedy raised difficult dynastic problems. Now none of George III's sons had legitimate children who might become heirs to the English throne. Three royal dukes (Clarence, Kent and Cambridge) were unmarried and hastily found themselves acceptable wives. The Duke of Clarence – later King William IV – had spent over twenty years of happy unmarried life with the talented London actress, Mrs Dorothy Jordan, who had given him ten children (the Fitzclarence family); but neither of his daughters by his marriage to Adelaide of Saxe-Meiningen lived for more than a few weeks. The Duke of Kent was more successful: he married Victoire (a sister of Leopold of Saxe-Coburg), and on 24 May 1819 became father of the future Queen Victoria. But the Duke died when the baby was eight months old, and in her childhood Victoria saw little of the Court life of either of her uncles, George IV or William IV. The formative influences on the young Victoria were therefore not so much Hanoverian as Coburg in origin, for after her husband's death the Duchess of Kent was largely dependent on her brother Leopold for advice.

George IV died in June 1830. The new ruler, William IV, was nicknamed 'Silly Billy', and knew it. For many years he had served in the Royal Navy and, although his career afloat was never conspicuously distinguished, he could claim to have been a friend through two decades of the great Nelson. William's bluff manner made him popular. He enjoyed walking and talking with his subjects, who were amused by his constant disregard of royal pomp. At first, politically, he was more sympathetic to the Whigs than George IV had been, either as Regent or King. In 1831–2 William supported the Reform Bill Prime Minister, Grey, when political feeling in the country was so intense that a more Tory-minded ruler might well have precipitated revolution. Later in the reign William showed that he believed parliamentary reform had gone far enough, and his treatment of Lord Melbourne (who succeeded Grey as leader of the Whigs) was, at times, casually abrupt. He disliked his sister-in-law the Duchess of Kent and (rightly) distrusted the influence upon the Duchess of her controller of the household, Sir John Conroy. William was determined (so he publicly remarked) to live long enough to prevent the Duchess from becoming Regent for Victoria. Despite failing health, his willpower triumphed. Victoria celebrated her eighteenth birthday in May 1837, the age at which she became constitutionally able to reign on her own. Twenty-seven days later William IV died.

The accession of Victoria meant a break in the dynastic link with Hanover, where no woman could succeed to the throne. The Duke of Cumberland duly became King George V of Hanover, which ceased to be of importance in British affairs for the first time in a century and a quarter. Victoria's new subjects cared little about Hanover anyhow. There was a rush of sentimental loyalty to their diminutive Queen. 'The very depth and fulness of his loyal attachment to his Queen ought to make a virtuous Englishman so much the more solicitous to protect her from perils of which it is scarcely in the nature of things that she should of herself be conscious', declared *The Times* on the morning after her accession. But if there was something refreshing about her political innocence, it was soon lost in the realities of government. Malicious reports of the Queen's unjust treatment of one of her ladies-in-waiting, Lady Flora Hastings, made Victoria temporarily so unpopular that she was received with hisses when she went to Ascot for the races in July 1839. Public opinion was excessively fickle, as she was to find on many occasions over the following six decades.

Queen Victoria reigned for nearly sixty-four years, longer than any other sovereign in English history and exceeded on the Continent only by Louis XIV in France (seventy-two years on the throne, but eight of them under a Regent) and Franz Josef of Austria-Hungary, who reigned for nearly sixty-eight years. Yet, in a sense, there were at least four Queen Victorias, each emphasizing different facets of her personality, though linked by the same self-willed determination of character which observers had noted in her girlhood.

The earliest of these four Victorias is a happily partisan young Whig, anxious to shake off the influence of her mother and eager to note down the opinions of her first Prime Minister, Melbourne, on everything from French and English literature to the fashion in caps and bonnets. Many of Melbourne's comments were intended to stimulate a mind which had never been taught to think and to question accepted views. The young Queen certainly had a romantic crush on this ablest of tutors, and gossips made much of her affection for a sophisticated father-figure who had twice been cited as co-respondent in divorce suits. Yet it was Melbourne who gave her confidence in herself, who showed her how different was the English constitutional monarchy from any continental model, and who imparted to this five-feet-tall 'slip of a girl', nervous and shy at heart, a sense of the royal past. 'Lord M . . . knows about everybody and everything', she wrote, and added, 'his conversations always improve one greatly'.

In 1839 Victoria fell in love with her cousin, Prince Albert of Saxe-Coburg-Gotha, who had been born three months after her. The marriage had been fostered over many years by Leopold of Saxe-Coburg, who was uncle to both Victoria and Albert (and, by now, King of the Belgians). Melbourne favoured the match, but it was

opposed in Parliament and was unpopular in London as a whole, partly because Albert was thought to be an impoverished German princeling on the make, and partly because it was felt that the influence of the small state of Coburg was already disproportionally large in English affairs. Victoria, however, was genuinely in love with her handsome and talented cousin; and the wedding took place in February 1840.

It was Prince Albert who created the second of the four Victorias, a Queen who seemed to her subjects virtuously domesticated and tirelessly conscientious in performing the official functions of royalty. In reality the Queen hated motherhood and continued to hold strong opinions on

The death of Nelson, the British Navy's most famous son, at Trafalgar.

Gent   No Gent   & Regent !!

Pub.d by T. Tegg Nº 111 Cheapside July 5.1816.

LEFT Subtlety was quite alien to the Regency period. This cartoon is aimed at the Prince Regent.

BELOW Exotic splendour in Sussex-by-the-sea. The banqueting room of the Prince Regent's architectural folly, the Brighton Pavilion.

Victoria and Albert, with the
aging Duke of Wellington
making a presentation to the
young Duke of Connaught on
his first birthday. Just discernible
behind the Duke's head is the
Crystal Palace in Hyde Park.

Wilkie's well-known portrait of the honest, dull William IV. Surprisingly enough, for twenty years before his marriage he lived with a famous London actress by whom he had a large number of children.

policies and politicians which frequently ran counter to the general feeling of the country. There were quarrels and disagreements between Victoria and Albert, sometimes over public events, sometimes over matters at Court and in the family; but none of these incidents was of serious importance. What mattered for Victorian England was the spectacle of a happily married Queen and consort who set an example of marital rectitude to the middle classes at a time of growing prosperity. Even the aristocracy accepted a moral lead from Buckingham Palace, although there were some who scoffed privately at the 'Albertine' smugness of the new-look monarchy, with its succession of four boys and five girls following one another through the royal nursery over a span of seventeen years.

Albert interested the Queen in matters which Melbourne had ignored – social questions, commerce, industry, the 'condition of the people'. He was an unusually gifted man himself: an artist, musician and composer; an earnest student of what was then called political economy; and a draughtsman capable of planning ideal homes for town labourers or extensions to Osborne, the new royal residence on the Isle of Wight. He was primarily responsible for the Great Exhibition of 1851, when six million people flocked to a 'crystal palace' of glass, erected by Joseph Paxton amid the elms of Hyde Park. Never before had science been harnessed to national prestige. The industrial revolution was bringing wealth to Britain, and the Exhibition celebrated the achievements of the land of

OPPOSITE A delightful portrait of the future Queen Victoria, then aged eleven.

RIGHT Victoria and Albert and their model Victorian family.

Albert's adoption. The Prince had to overcome opposition from many quarters before the Exhibition was ready for the Queen to open on May Day, 1851. It was, Victoria wrote in her private journal, 'one of the greatest and most glorious days of our lives with which, to my pride and joy, the name of my dearly beloved Albert is forever associated'. She would have liked her husband appointed 'King Consort', but Parliament was uncooperative. Eventually in 1857, the compromise dignity of 'Prince Consort' was bestowed on Albert.

Under her husband's guidance the Queen forgot her earlier Whig enthusiasms and came to appreciate the merits of such moderate Tories as Sir Robert Peel. Both Victoria and Albert were constantly on strained relations with Lord Palmerston, whose jauntily independent conduct of diplomacy seemed dangerous to the Prince. In 1854 Britain and France became involved in war with

Russia, a conflict known from the main theatre of operations as the Crimean War. Albert had hoped to control the hotheads in the Cabinet, and regretted his failure. Victoria deplored the drift into war, but was proud of the bearing of her troops. She could not avoid the appointment of Palmerston as a war leader and approved of his handling of the eventual peace negotiations. But the Prince Consort was still worried by his diplomatic methods. In December 1861 there seemed a danger of conflict between Britain and the United States, partly because of Palmerston's sympathies with the Confederates in the Civil War. An American warship removed two diplomatic envoys of the southern Confederates from a British ship, the *Trent*, sailing to England. The vigorous protests of the Palmerston Government alarmed the Prince Consort, who was feverishly ill at Windsor with typhoid. He rose from his sickbed early on 1 December, staggered to his desk and

Continued on pg 132

RIGHT The Anti-Slavery Convention, 1840. British and other colonial interests had long made slavery profitable, but there were many who campaigned zealously against it.

BELOW A Christmas card made by NCOS of the Coldstream Guards and presented to their commanding officer during the Boer War – a far cry from the log fires and rich food of an Edwardian Christmas.

ABOVE In Birmingham or Bombay, Frinton or Fiji, the Queen-Empress's effigy speeded her loyal subjects' letters on their way.

In 1584 Sir Walter Raleigh fitted out an expedition which staked a claim for Elizabeth I to an island off what is now North Carolina. This venture, though unsuccessful, marked the inauguration of an overseas empire which grew throughout the Stuart era and the Cromwellian inter-regnum. Settlements sprang up along the seaboard from Newfoundland through Massachusetts to Virginia, in the West Indies, on the Indian sub-continent, and in the Malay archipelago. A climax was reached with the victories of 1759 in French Canada, but this first British Empire was soon after virtually destroyed by the American struggle for independence.

The second British Empire took shape during the Napoleonic Wars. It rested upon the old settlements of the East India Company and on the Canadian colonies, adding to it new acquisitions in southern Africa, Ceylon and islands in the oceans, together with the settlements opened up by exploration in Australia and New Zealand. By 1830 English patriotic writers felt justified in appropriating the boast of sixteenth-century Spain, claiming for their sovereign 'dominions on which the sun never sets'.

Growth of Empire became an outstanding feature of Victoria's reign. There were four main reasons for this development: British-manufactured goods needed markets; a surplus population needed new sources of food and raw materials and living space for emigrants; steam power on sea and land led to improved communications; and the growth of medical knowledge made it gradually possible to settle in previously unhealthy regions.

The climax of Britain's imperialism came in the 1880s and 1890s when a powerful fleet patrolled the seas from Plymouth to Gibraltar, Malta, Alexandria, Bombay, Trincomalee, Singapore and Hong Kong. Cecil Rhodes, as Prime Minister of Cape Colony from 1890 to 1896, dreamt of a 'Cape to Cairo' railway which would run under British control from Egypt to South Africa. This ambition was nearly realized after the First World War; but it brought Britain to the verge of war with France at Fashoda on the upper Nile in 1898, it hardened feelings towards the British in Berlin, and it helped to deepen the antagonism between the colonialists of British descent and the Boer settlers, with their differing traditions and beliefs.

The British Empire was never a philanthropic under-taking. It was a business proposition which paid good dividends in Victorian England and Scotland. At times the sight of a globe on which (as Chesterton wrote) 'the spots are all red and the rest is all grey' evoked a vulgarly nationalistic pride. Occasionally weak soldiers and officials committed errors tragic in their consequences for hundreds of men, women and children. But there was also a long line of imperial proconsuls who believed in sound government and administration.

BELOW Palmerston, the apostle of gun-boat diplomacy.

BELOW The Royal Family opening the Great Exhibition – Albert's brain-child – at the Crystal Palace in 1851. Exhibitors and viewers came from all over the world, and England could truly be said to be the hub of the universe.

BELOW Troops of the Heavy Brigade relax in camp in the Crimea, 1855. A rare picture by the pioneer of war photo-graphy, Roger Fenton.

LEFT Establishment and dignity –
Victoria and her Prince Consort
in 1861.

OPPOSITE The widow of
Windsor and grandmother of
Europe, photographed in 1899.
The children are Prince Edward,
Prince Albert (seated), Princess
Mary and Prince Henry.

toned down a despatch to Washington, so as to secure the release of the envoys and a peaceful solution. But Albert never sat at his desk again. The strain was too great. He died shortly before midnight on 14 December, eight months short of his forty-third birthday.

The Queen suffered a severe nervous collapse from the shock of Albert's death. The third of the four Victorias is the 'widow of Windsor', a recluse wrapped in mourning clothes, still going diligently through the paperwork of constitutional monarchy, but declining all public func-

tions, even delegating the official opening of Parliament to the Prince of Wales. Much of her time she would spend at Balmoral, the Scottish Highland home purchased on the tenth anniversary of her accession. There she became dependent on a bluntly spoken but kindly and strong Scottish personal servant, John Brown. This curiously isolated existence led to tales in the foreign press that the Queen had secretly married Brown and even to the growth of republican sentiment in London by the early 1870s. It was argued that the monarchy had become an

expensive anachronism, fulfilling no useful or decorative task.

By now a major political change had taken place. The old labels, Whig and Tory, were out of date. Organized political parties, Liberal and Conservative, had taken their place, led respectively by William Gladstone and Benjamin Disraeli. The Queen respected Gladstone's reforming zeal but she found some of his measures unpalatable and his manner tedious: 'Mr Gladstone', she once remarked 'addresses me as though I were a public meeting.' But Disraeli flattered her. Confidential reports bore the mark of his lively pen, which had already written ten novels. During Disraeli's government of 1874–80 Victoria enjoyed her Prime Minister's company in a way she had not known since the days of Melbourne. She actually invited Disraeli to sit down in her presence, an honour which, on the first occasion it was offered, he declined with judicious modesty.

The fourth Victoria, a matriarchal Empress, was in part a creation of Disraeli. She was also the fulfilment of her subjects' need for a symbolic figure whom they could revere with pride. In 1876 Disraeli – later that summer he became Lord Beaconsfield – steered a Royal Titles Bill through Parliament; and in January 1877 Victoria was proclaimed Empress of India. This was a dignity she relished. In old age she came to delight in everything Indian, adding a Durbar Room to Osborne House which was even more incongruously oriental beside the Solent than her uncle's Pavilion at Brighton.

It was not only to the Indian sub-continent that Victoria's authority was extended. The closing decades of the century saw a Great Power 'scramble for Africa', with the British securing the largest share. Under Lord Salisbury, Conservative Prime Minister for twelve of the last fifteen years of her reign, the Queen became sovereign over a sixth of the world's land-surface; and this Empire was protected by a Royal Navy more powerful than the combined fleets of any other two nations. The heyday of British imperialism fell on 20 June 1897 when Captain Ames, 'the tallest officer in the British Army', led the Diamond Jubilee Procession through London to St. Paul's. There, outside the cathedral, Victoria's open landau halted. Regiments from Canada, Australia, New Zealand, Cape Colony, with Bengal Lancers and British redcoats and bluejackets, joined the Londoners in celebrating her long 'dominion over palm and pine'. The oaks and elms of Kensington Palace, where sixty years before a girl in a dressing gown learnt of her accession, seemed parochially remote at such a climax to her reign.

Victoria's last year was overshadowed by war in South Africa between her army and the Boers beyond the Orange and Vaal rivers. The struggle against these farmer-settlers

of Dutch origin made Britain unpopular, and the Queen was abused in German and French newspapers. But Victoria's personal influence in the Courts of Europe was strong enough to deter the gathering of a hostile coalition. The eldest son of her eldest daughter was German Emperor, a granddaughter was Empress of All the Russias. Other granddaughters were married to the heirs of Greece and Romania, a first cousin reigned in Belgium, and there were close links with the royal family of Denmark and many smaller German dynasties. Letters of congratulation, condolence, reproof and sometimes gossip sped out from Windsor, Osborne and Balmoral alike to great palaces in Berlin and St Petersburg or the castles and residences of minor German royalty. When at last the 'grandmother of Europe' died at Osborne on 22 January 1901 there were at her bedside the reigning German Emperor and the two successors to her royal and imperial crowns.

Nineteenth-century British politics were dominated by two great figures – Gladstone and Disraeli. Victoria and Gladstone had incompatible personalities, but the smooth and silky Disraeli cajoled, flattered and, as a result, influenced her.

9
The People's Kings
1901~1952

This dashing portrait of Edward VII was taken in 1875, when he still had twenty-five years ahead of him as Prince of Wales.

E DWARD VII was born in November 1841 and was therefore already in his sixtieth year at his accession. He was baptized Albert Edward, and called, within the family circle, 'Bertie'. But even before his christening he had been created Prince of Wales, the title by which he was known throughout the British Empire and in Europe. He travelled more than any of his predecessors; to the United States and Canada; to India, Palestine, Turkey and Egypt; three times to Russia, and frequently to the western European countries. Some of this journeying was prompted by frustration, since Victoria refused to allow him any political activities at home, and only in the last eight years of her life was he allowed to read Foreign Office documents and despatches. It was natural he should be interested in foreign affairs. His favourite sister, 'Vicky', who was eleven months his senior, married into the Prussian Royal House and became German Empress in 1888; and the Prince's own bride, Alexandra, was a Danish Princess with family connections as widespread as those of Queen Victoria herself.

It was difficult to be an eldest son of 'Albert the Good'. The Prince Consort set Bertie an impossibly high standard in scholastic attainment and moral rectitude; and inevitably found him a disappointment in both. No English prince had attended a university before, and the few terms spent by Bertie at Oxford and Cambridge were a novelty, even though academically valueless. The Prince of Wales seemed, however, to have more of the character of his Hanoverian great-uncles than of his father. There was a long list of liaisons with actresses and society beauties, most of them after the Prince Consort's death. Queen Victoria deplored her son's involvement in a divorce action and as a witness to a scandal over gambling at cards. His behaviour was out of keeping with the prevalent facade of middle-class respectability. More than once he was rebuked, heavy-handedly, in the columns of *The Times*, and there was a censorious tone even in the leading article at his accession.

Edward VII – the first king seen with a beard since Charles I – was popular with most of his subjects. They

Max Beerbohm's satire on the uneasy relationship between the Queen and her eldest son and heir. The cartoon, entitled 'The rare, and rather awful visits of Albert Edward, Prince of Wales, to Windsor Castle' comes from *Things Old and New*.

OPPOSITE George V and Queen Mary, with two of their children, painted by Lavery at Buckingham Palace.

'Or walk with Kings – nor lose the common touch'. George V admires a cabbage grown on allotments on Clapham Common in 1918.

liked his geniality and tact; they were glad of a sovereign whose horses won the classic races; and they were amused by his girth, reputedly a constant forty-eight inches round the waist. He was said to be sensitive about his figure and once, as a gesture to his physicians, limited himself to one small cigar before breakfast and a single brandy after dinner. In the rest of the day, however, he smoked up to twelve large cigars and twenty cigarettes, enjoyed champagne in moderation, and ate five substantial meals including normally a twelve-course dinner. His appetite seems to have been slightly in excess of the Prince Regent's, although his consumption of wines was comparatively low.

Politically Edward's reign was almost evenly divided between Conservative and Liberal governments. The Conservatives were in office until December 1905, first under Salisbury and, then, from 1902, under his nephew, Arthur Balfour. These were years of relative quiet in domestic affairs but with an important change in foreign policy, the creation of the *Entente Cordiale* between Britain and France in 1904. This agreement was not an alliance, but it provided for collaboration between two nations traditionally hostile to one another over the centuries. Edward VII played a considerable role in easing the tension between the two countries, notably by a visit to Paris in May 1903. As the procession rode down the Champs Elysees on arrival, Edward heard shouts, not just

of '*Vivent les Boers*', but of '*Vive Jeanne d'Arc*' as well; but Paris was a city of which he had long been fond, and his tact and kindly gestures ensured that, as he left, the crowd was chanting the French equivalent of 'Long live good old Edward!'

The Liberal government of Campbell-Bannerman won a large majority in the 1906 General Election and carried through a series of domestic reforms which were continued by Campbell-Bannerman's successor, Asquith, who took over as Prime Minister in April 1908. Edward was never so politically partisan as his mother, and he welcomed some Liberal measures, including the introduction of old age pensions; but he was alarmed by what he considered the radical attitude of the younger Liberals, especially Lloyd George and Winston Churchill. In the last year of the King's life there was a constitutional crisis, caused by the Conservative majority in the Lords throwing out Lloyd George's 'People's Budget' of 1909. Asquith wanted to reduce the power of the House of Lords, a measure which he believed required the creation of sufficient Liberal peers to overcome the 'die-hard Tories' of the upper House. Edward disliked such a step and sought a compromise. He could not shake off the social habits of a lifetime and these, together with the political strain, weakened his heart. He died late in the evening of 6 May 1910. The last piece of news of which he was conscious

Continued on pg 142

Great Britain has spent ten years of the present century fighting major wars. In the First World War (1914–8) the principal Allies, besides the British Empire, were France, Russia, Belgium, Serbia, Italy, Japan, Greece, Romania and, from April 1917, the USA. They fought against the Central Powers – Germany, Austria-Hungary, Turkey and Bulgaria.

The immediate cause of the First World War was the assassination of the heir to the Austrian throne by a Serbian nationalist in Sarajevo on 28 June 1914. The Austrians declared war on Serbia a month later. Russia supported Serbia, while treaties bound Germany to assist Austria and France to assist Russia. German war plans against France required the passage of troops through Belgium, who appealed for help to Britain. Technically it was in answer to this appeal that Britain declared war on Germany on 4 August 1914. But the ultimate cause of the war lies further back, notably in the division of Europe into two armed camps, an alliance system originally defensive in character. Anglo-German friction arose from trade rivalry (especially in Africa and the Middle East) and from suspicion in London of the new and large German fleet.

The decisive battle zone of the First World War was the Western Front which, from the end of 1914, was stabilized for almost three years along defensive trenches covering 200 miles from the Belgian coast to Verdun. A more fluid war was fought in Russian Poland and the Ukraine. Against Turkey the principal front was in Palestine, after the failure of the British and Australasian attempt to seize the Gallipoli Peninsula in 1915. Land fighting also took place in Macedonia, north-eastern Italy, south-western Africa and present-day Iraq and Tanzania. The main Anglo-German naval battle was at Jutland (31 May 1916). The war, which ended on 11 November 1918, saw the first use of poison gas, tanks, aircraft and submarines.

The Second World War (fought primarily against the Axis allies – Germany, Italy and Japan) had its origins in Hitler's unwillingness to accept the frontiers imposed on Germany in 1919. Britain and France went to war with Germany on 3 September 1939 to honour treaty commitments to Poland, invaded by Germany two days before. The war differed considerably from its predecessor. Allied armies were virtually excluded from western Europe between France's fall in June 1940 and the D-day landings in Normandy four years later. From 1941 onwards the most terrible battles were on the Russian Front; but the fighting was in general world-wide, with campaigns in North Africa and (after December 1941) in the Pacific and in Burma. Civilian suffering was greater, partly because of concentrated bombing, partly through the effects of enemy occupation. In Europe war ended with Germany's unconditional surrender in May 1945. Japan fought on for three more months but surrendered after the Americans had dropped atomic bombs on Hiroshima and Nagasaki.

The First World War left 17 million dead, one million of them subjects of the King-Emperor George V. Soviet dead alone in the Second World War outnumbered the previous war's casualties. Total casualties of the Second World War are estimated at 37 million. About half a million of the dead came from the British Commonwealth.

Ammunition is brought by horse to the forward lines on the Somme in the winter of 1916. This was the last war to use horses to any extent.

RIGHT The First World War brought women an opportunity to leave the confines of their homes. Here munitions workers are turning shells.

LEFT After the devastation of one war, Britain was eager to avoid another. Chamberlain and the French premier signed away the Sudetenland at the Munich Peace Conference, but this was not to keep Hitler and Mussolini happy for long.

RIGHT Churchill played an active part in the war; his staff were hard-pressed to keep him out of danger zones. Here he visits the Western Desert in 1942.

LEFT Churchill and the Royal Family wave joyfully from the Palace balcony on VE Day, when London exploded with jubilant crowds.

RIGHT Bombs fall on Bremen. RAF air supremacy was an important factor in the fall of Germany.

BELOW LEFT Women again play their part in war: the Land Army took the place of the workers away fighting.

BELOW Tanks and other armoured vehicles had replaced horses on the battle front – here a German tank crew surrenders to British infantry in 1942.

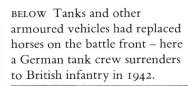

King George V and Queen
Mary in 1917, on board the
royal train.

was conveyed to him by his heir at five that afternoon: his
horse had won the Spring Plate at Kempton Park by half
a length. 'I am very glad', he said. It was a fitting exit line.

For two centuries the relationship between sovereign
and heir to the British crown had been strained. But in
1910 the new ruler, George V, could truthfully write in his
diary, 'I have lost my best friend and the best of fathers.'
Throughout Edward VII's reign, his heir had worked
closely with him. He knew the nature of the current
political problems, as well as the personalities in public
life. George V was trained as a naval officer and retained
throughout life an enthusiasm for sailing and the sea. He
was less sophisticated than his father, whose love of continental Europe he certainly never shared. George disliked
change and distrusted fashion, being unable to distinguish
between a passing trend and a social innovation of real
significance. Fortunately, in 1893, he married Princess Mary
of Teck. Although one grandmother was a Hungarian
countess, the future Queen Mary was a Londoner by
birth, a granddaughter of the Duke of Cambridge,
youngest of George III's sons to survive infancy. She was
by no means an intellectual, but she was better educated
than her husband; her mental initiative was greater and
she was less rigid in outlook. While George V was made
irritable by what he could not understand, Queen Mary
frequently showed herself sympathetic to a widening of
experience. Without her, George could easily have become
a crowned country squire cut off from his people, an
anglicized version of Tsar Nicholas II, the first cousin
whom in appearance he so resembled. Edward VII had by
nature a genial, popular touch; but it was Queen Mary
who made George V a people's King.

Yet George, again the well-trained naval officer,
possessed a self-demanding concept of duty. All these
qualities may be seen in the persistence with which he
tackled the two major internal crises of his early years on
the throne. He warned Asquith against cheapening the
monarch's bestowal of honours by requiring the creation
of Liberal peers in order to settle the constitutional problems
of the Lords, unresolved in Edward's reign; but, after two
elections had given the Liberals a majority, the King made
it clear that he would, if necessary, support Asquith. And
it was on George V's initiative that an inter-party conference gathered in Buckingham Palace in the summer of
1914 to try to prevent Ulster's opposition on Irish Home
Rule turning into a protracted civil war.

Such disputes were soon overshadowed by the coming
of the First World War. 'It is a terrible catastrophe but it is
not our fault', the King wrote in his journal on 4 August,
1914, the day Britain declared war on Germany. At the
same time his cousin in Berlin, Kaiser Wilhelm II, was

RIGHT The sailor king –
George v at the helm of the
royal yacht *Britannia*.

ABOVE The very straight-faced
pomp of Edwardian cere-
monial – peers and peeresses
cluster round Edward VII,
Queen Alexandra and the future
George v at Edward's
coronation.

OPPOSITE A royal family at home – George VI, Queen Elizabeth (now the Queen Mother), Princess Margaret and Princess Elizabeth (now Elizabeth II) take tea. The somnolent corgi completes the scene.

RIGHT The news breaks, after months of British press silence enforced mainly by Lord Beaverbrook, who passionately hoped abdication could be averted.

blaming 'George and Nicky' (the Tsar) 'for playing me false', adding 'If my grandmother had been alive, she would never have allowed it.' In reality, of course, the rivalry of the Great Powers, accentuated in Anglo-German relations by the Kaiser's desire for a large 'High Seas Fleet', went far beyond any sentiment of dynastic consanguinity. George V had, on several occasions, told his cousin that if France joined Russia in a war with Germany, it was likely that 'we shall be dragged into it', but in Berlin more attention was given to the King's professed hope that war would be avoided than to his warning.

Under the impact of anti-German sentiment George V resolved, in 1917, to change the name of the dynasty from Saxe-Coburg-Gotha to Windsor. This was a personal decision and not forced on the King by any disloyalty within the empire. He spent the war years endlessly visiting troops, seamen, airfields and factories; he supported and advised his two wartime Prime Ministers, Asquith and Lloyd George, and although he played some part in the appointment of senior commanders, he was careful not to intrigue. While visiting the British Expeditionary Force in France during October 1915 he was thrown from his horse and fractured his pelvis. He was brought home on a hospital-ship; and, in a heavy sea, suffered considerably. It was a serious accident for a man of fifty, and he never fully recovered his physical strength.

Prince Albert and Prince Henry, later George VI and the Duke of Gloucester, at Loch Muick in 1907.

With the return of peace his long experience was of great value to a new generation. In the continental land empires– Russia, Germany, Austria-Hungary–war and defeat led to revolutions which destroyed the monarchical order. In Britain the common suffering of a four-year struggle lowered social barriers less dramatically, but there was widespread change. Democratic socialism spread rapidly; women over thirty received the vote; many occupations and professions ceased to be exclusively male; popular motoring and cheaper transport 'opened up' the country, while broadcasting and the cinema offered new forms of entertainment. Some of these changes had effects on the monarchy. Newsreels made the King and Queen better known; so, indeed, did the motor-cars. George V's voice – gruff but warmly avuncular – was heard 'over the air' on nineteen occasions between April 1924 and his death, nearly twelve years later. To many millions he thus became a living person, not merely a profile on a coin.

Politically the King was helped by his Private Secretaries at Buckingham Palace. They assisted him, for example, over the difficult decision in 1923 when, on the resignation of the Conservative Prime Minister Bonar Law, the King summoned the relatively unknown Stanley Baldwin to succeed him because he was a member of the Commons whereas the rival candidate, Lord Curzon, was a peer. It was argued that it would be difficult for a Prime Minister to lead the government effectively from the Lords if

Labour (virtually unrepresented in the Upper House) was the leading opposition party.

A few months later George V was faced with yet another Prime Minister. On the twenty-third anniversary of 'dear Grandmama's' death (as he wryly noted) the King invited Ramsay Macdonald to form the first Labour Government. George's relations with the Labour politicians were cordial; he took pains to put them at their ease. In June 1929 a second Labour government was formed, and Margaret Bondfield (Minister of Labour) became the first woman sworn of the Privy Council, taking the oath in the King's presence at Windsor. There were, however, problems of readjustment for the King. In October 1929 he resented having to receive a Soviet envoy, 'an ambassador of a government which, if it did not connive at, did not disapprove of, the brutal murder of his favourite first cousins'–so his Private Secretary phrased the royal complaint to the Foreign Office. But, characteristically, in the end George V accepted as duty this personally disagreeable exercise in diplomatic courtesy, and shook hands with a Soviet ambassador on 27 March 1930.

The King fervently believed in Britain's imperial mission. In 1911 he travelled to India with Queen Mary and received homage as Emperor from his Indian peoples at a durbar in Delhi. After the war ill health curtailed his visits overseas but he was represented, round the world, by his two eldest sons; and he continued to take a personal

LEFT The Duke and Duchess of Windsor photographed by Cecil Beaton on their wedding day, 3 June 1937, at the Château de Condé, France.

BELOW The Duke and Duchess of York leave their wedding reception in 1923, to wild acclaim from the crowd.

interest in the gradual growth of self-governing institutions within the Empire.

Soon afterwards, on 20 January 1936, he died at his favourite home, 'dear old Sandringham', in Norfolk. His successor, Edward VIII, was a bachelor of forty-one, who looked still under thirty. Since the war, in which he served with the army in France and Egypt, he had enjoyed the adulation normally reserved for a matinee idol, and was deservedly popular in his principality of Wales. Within a few months of his accession the foreign press linked his name with Mrs Wallis Simpson, an American two years younger than himself. The King's desire to marry Mrs Simpson brought him into conflict with the Prime Minister, Baldwin, as well as with the Archbishop of Canterbury, and the influential editor of The Times, Geoffrey Dawson. They opposed the marriage, not because Mrs Simpson was a commoner born in America, but because she had been twice divorced, and it seemed difficult to reconcile her marriage to the King with his responsibilities as titular 'Supreme Governor' of the Church of England. Rather than give up 'the woman I love', Edward VIII abdicated and went into voluntary exile on 11 December 1936. He was created Duke of Windsor, married Mrs Simpson at the French chateau of Condé in June 1937, and visited Austria and Germany, paying a courtesy call on Hitler at Berchtesgaden in October.

Edward VIII reigned for three hundred and twenty-four days uncrowned. Arrangements had been made for his coronation on 12 May 1937. The coronation date remained; but the crown was now placed on the head of his brother, the Duke of York, who had come to the throne as George VI. This third king in a little over a year was, like his father, trained as a naval officer. He fought at Jutland in 1916 and subsequently learnt to fly, receiving his wings in the newly constituted RAF in 1919. As Duke of York he attracted less limelight than his elder brother, but he became deeply interested in labour conditions and in 1921 started an annual 'Duke of York Camp' where young workers and public schoolboys could live together side by side, free from inhibiting class barriers. The Duke's marriage in 1923 to Lady Elizabeth Bowes-Lyon was popular, not least because the Duchess brought to London society the grace of the old Scottish nobility.

George VI was a man of courage and dedication. Throughout his life he had been forced to fight against a stammer, an impediment he had almost conquered before he made his first broadcast as King. But, apart from this disability, he suffered from a lack of acquaintance with documents of State and, indeed, knew few politicians personally. Unfortunately he had come to the throne under the steadily lengthening shadows of international crisis. Within sixteen months of his coronation, air raid trenches were being dug in London when Hitler's threat to Czechoslovakia brought Europe to the verge of war. George VI was relieved when his Prime Minister, Neville Chamberlain, reached agreement with Hitler during this 'Munich Crisis' of September 1938, but he soon realized there was little hope of a lasting peace. In May and June 1939 the King and Queen crossed the Atlantic, partly to see Canada, but also to strengthen the Anglo-American connection. George VI became the first reigning British sovereign to set foot on the soil of the USA, and he established a warm friendship with President Roosevelt. The royal couple stayed informally with the President at his home only twelve weekends before Hitler's invasion of Poland unleashed the Second World War.

The King, like his father a quarter of a century earlier, visited his services at home and overseas. He went to France, to North Africa and to Malta. But it was a different type of war. Air raids levelled many cities in Britain, which duly received royal visits of sympathetic encouragement. This identification of King and people was psychologically of great importance in 'the year we stood alone'. Buckingham Palace received, in all, nine direct hits, the worst occasion being on 12 September 1940 when two small bombs fell in a courtyard about a hundred feet from the room in which the King was sitting. At first he held inner reservations about Churchill's impetuosity but by the end of 1940 he fully recognized his stature as a war leader. Sovereign and Prime Minister normally discussed the progress of operations at an informal luncheon every Tuesday. There were passing disagreements, notably over the plan to land in Normandy in 1944, but each respected the other's views. Occasionally Churchill allowed himself to be restrained by the King's counsel.

Labour's electoral victory in 1945 surprised the King. He thought the people 'very ungrateful' to Churchill; but he found his own constitutional position strengthened because he represented continuity and experience. Apart from the Prime Minister (Attlee) only four members of the government had sat in a Cabinet. It was partly on the King's advice that Attlee offered the Foreign Office to Ernest Bevin. In a private letter the King admitted he did not find all the Labour ministers 'easy to talk to'; and, at times, he urged Attlee to slow down projects of nationalization. He accepted as inevitable the spread of self-government in the Indian sub-continent but he was saddened by the communal strife, and personally regretted his loss of the title of Emperor (August 1947).

His final years were cheered by the marriage of his elder daughter to Lieutenant Philip Mountbatten but his health deteriorated rapidly in 1949–50 and in September 1951 he underwent an operation for cancer. On 6 February 1952 he died in his sleep at Sandringham.

George VI, as Duke of York, holds the baby Princess Elizabeth.
At her birth no one ever thought she would one day be queen.

Epilogue
The New Elizabethans

AT her accession, Queen Elizabeth II was in Kenya with her husband, the Duke of Edinburgh, at the the start of a five-month tour of Africa, Ceylon, Australia and New Zealand. She returned to London immediately and was met by members of her Privy Council headed by Winston Churchill, back as Conservative Prime Minister again after gaining a small parliamentary majority in the General Election of October 1951. A battery of cameras caught the poignancy of this moment, as the twenty-five-year-old sovereign climbed down the aircraft steps to be received by a statesman who had entered Parliament in the reign of her great-great-grandmother.

Inevitably in the following months the press and radio began to talk of the 'New Elizabethan' Age. Probably this trend reflected a mood of wish-fulfilment, a weariness with many years of austerity, together with regret at the evident decline in Britain's stature as a world power. This sentiment reached a climax with the coronation on 2 June 1953, an event heralded by the auspicious overnight news that a team of Commonwealth climbers had at last conquered Mount Everest. The coronation service in Westminster Abbey was filmed and televised, for the first time: 'The eyes of millions will be upon Her Majesty – for the marvel of television will annihilate distance and range far-off multitudes with the congregation in the Abbey', the coronation number of the *Radio Times* declared. Representatives from seventy countries came to London for the coronation, and although it was a miserably wet day, hearts warmed readily to the principals in the ceremony and the procession.

Elizabeth II's reign was to become an age of adaptation to a far greater extent than even the second half of her grandfather's reign. Nothing changed so drastically as the relationship between the crown and the Empire overseas. The old centralized relationship had gone even before the Queen's accession; and from 1949 onwards it was accepted that a country might adopt a republican form of government and yet remain within the British Commonwealth.

There was, however, a certain ambiguity over the sovereign's status. This was emphasized by the formal title with which she was hailed at her coronation: 'Elizabeth II, by the Grace of God, of Great Britain and Northern Ireland and of her other Realms and Territories, Queen, Head of the Commonwealth, Defender of the Faith'. It has been her constant concern to clarify and strengthen the loose constitutional role implied by this designedly vague formula. No collective noun has appeared so frequently in her speeches as 'Commonwealth'. The Queen has always been anxious to ensure that her overseas subjects came to regard the crown as an adjunct of democratic rule rather than as a piece of autocratic hardware. Probably the change in the last twenty years has been greater than she, or her advisers, anticipated; for by 1975 there were actually more republics within the Commonwealth than there were territories which acknowledged the Queen as their direct sovereign. Throughout these years the one institution which has remained popular within the Commonwealth, and acquired additional significance, is the crown. The Queen is the visible and human aspect of a unique association of governments.

Much of this personal success of the monarchy comes from the nature of the Commonwealth tours, which have become a regular feature of the reign. Both Princess Elizabeth and Princess Margaret accompanied their parents to South Africa in 1947 on the type of royal tour which Edward VIII and George VI had undertaken in the 1920s. But the Queen's travels from 1954 onwards have been rather different. Each seems to have shown less rigidity than before, less concern for protocol, less emphasis upon the monarchy as something 'made in England'. By 1959 the Queen and the Duke of Edinburgh were able to walk about informally on a visit to Newfoundland. These 'walkabouts' became increasingly common during the Australian visit of 1963. Some overseas tours, notably to Ghana in November 1961 and to Quebec in October 1964, were dangerous because of internal tensions. All were necessarily exhausting; but they have been important in

ABOVE A most solemn moment during the coronation of Queen Elizabeth II.

RIGHT The Queen and Prince Phillip chatting to some of the islanders at Gan in the Maldive Islands in the Indian Ocean which they visited in March 1972. They were the first Royal visitors to this remote group of islands.

ABOVE Prince Charles in the cockpit of a helicopter before take-off in September 1974. This was the start of a three-month course in Somerset.

RIGHT Photographed at Windsor for the royal silver wedding, 31 October 1972. Back row, standing left to right: the Earl of Snowdon; the Duke of Kent; Prince Michael of Kent; the Duke of Edinburgh; the Earl of St Andrews (elder son of the Duke of Kent); Prince Charles, the Prince of Wales; Prince Andrew; Hon. Angus Ogilvy and (extreme right) his son, James Ogilvy. Seated on chairs, left to right: Princess Margaret, Countess of Snowdon; the Duchess of Kent (holding Lord Nicholas Windsor, her younger son); Queen Elizabeth the Queen Mother; Queen Elizabeth II; Princess Anne; Marina Ogilvy, and her mother, Princess Alexandra. Seated on floor, left to right: Lady Sarah Armstrong-Jones; Viscount Linley (the two children of Princess Margaret); Prince Edward; Lady Helen Windsor (daughter of the Duke of Kent).

giving a sense of local possession of the crown: thus it was the Queen of Canada – not the Queen *in* Canada – who opened the St Lawrence Seaway in June 1959. And it was the Queen of Australia who opened the Sydney Opera House in 1974.

As well as these long periods of residence in the Commonwealth countries, the Queen and her husband have continued the practice begun by Queen Victoria in 1855 of making State Visits to foreign capitals. The growing integration of the European Economic Community increases the significance of such tours within Europe. When the Queen arrived in Bonn in May 1965 she became the first British sovereign to visit Germany since her grandparents went to the wedding of the Kaiser's daughter in May 1913. The Queen created a precedent in October 1972 when she was the guest of President Tito of Yugoslavia, a communist country. But the State Visits have not been confined to Europe: the Queen and the Duke have also been to the United States, to Mexico, Latin America, Iran and Japan. Yet the Queen still spends most

of each year within the United Kingdom, at Buckingham Palace, Windsor, Balmoral, Sandringham and, for a week each summer, at Holyroodhouse in Edinburgh.

The Duke of Edinburgh has greatly assisted the monarchy to adapt itself to the second half of the century. He introduced his Award Scheme for young people in 1955, a project intended to encourage enterprise and initiative in leisure-time pursuits; and in July 1956 the Duke convened in Oxford the first of his top-level conferences on industry. Prince Philip's jocular manner, his readiness to appear on television and to play cricket and polo on Sundays showed that he had none of the Prince Consort's stuffiness, even if, like Albert the Good, he was frequently concerned with science and industry.

The uncertainties of the Second World War had made it impossible for Princess Elizabeth or Princess Margaret to be educated at a school or university. But no attempt has been made to segregate, educationally, the four children of the Queen. Prince Charles, born in 1948, took his 'O' and 'A' Level examinations like any other boy among the

four hundred at Gordonstoun School. His brother Prince Andrew, born in 1960, entered Gordonstoun in 1973 and no doubt Prince Edward, born in 1964, will follow his example. From Gordonstoun Prince Charles went up to Trinity College, Cambridge, where he studied archaeology and modern history and became the first heir to the throne to take the full three-year Tripos examinations. He also showed a flair for amateur theatricals. Only with these qualifications behind him did he see service in the army, learn to fly, and eventually take command of a warship.

Princess Anne, born in 1950, also sat her 'O' and 'A' Level examinations, and was a boarder at Benenden School. She achieved distinction as a horsewoman and in 1971 won the European championship in the three-day equestrian event. Two years later she again rode in the championships, held that year in Kiev. Prince Philip also flew out to the Soviet Union for the competition. Thus, by a curious twist of history, two direct descendants of the Empress Catherine the Great were guests of the communist authorities in the Ukrainian capital where the Empress had made her famous triumphal entry in 1787. Two months later Princess Anne married Captain Mark Phillips, a horseman who was a member of the British team which won a gold medal at the 1972 Munich Olympics.

'A family on the throne is an interesting idea. It brings down the pride of sovereignty to the level of petty life.' So, in 1867, wrote Walter Bagehot, the great anatomist of the British Constitution. Almost exactly a century later the emphasis upon the family aspect of the monarchy reached a climax with close collaboration between Buckingham Palace and BBC Television. In June 1969 Richard Cawston's long documentary film gave the public in the United Kingdom and overseas an opportunity to follow through twelve months of the royal family's activities, both public and – within limits of discretion – private, too. The practice of showing 'public faces in private places' has now become so accepted that it is interesting to remember how, in 1953, the BBC was at first refused permission to televise the ceremonies of the coronation inside the Abbey. There are two dangers in this

The Queen, her Prime Minister, Harold Wilson, and her
Commonwealth Prime Ministers, in June 1965.

highly public presentation of the monarchy. The first is
that self-identification with the sovereign's family life will
accentuate the degree of partisan feeling over questions
which are not, strictly speaking, of general concern. The
second danger is that, in emphasizing the egalitarian
character of the monarchy, the Queen's advisers may
dispel the aura of accumulated history. The same Bagehot
who commended the values of domesticity around a
throne also warned his readers, 'We must not bring in the
daylight upon magic.' Fortunately so long as the ancient
orders of chivalry retain their ceremonies, and so long as
the sessions of Parliament open with their traditional
pageantry, there is little risk that the romantic mystery of
monarchy will pass into oblivion.

The Queen personifies an intangible quality of continuity with the past. She is a direct descendant of eighteen
English sovereigns since the Norman Conquest: William
the Conqueror himself; the first two Henrys; John;
Henry III; the first four Edwards; Henry VII; James I; the
first three Georges; Victoria; Edward VII; and George V
and his second son. She can trace her descent further back
through Alfred the Great to Egbert and the earliest
Kings of Wessex and, in the Scottish line, to Shakespeare's
Duncan and beyond. Not all these ancestors were com-
mendably virtuous or especially wise – hereditary kingship has always been a supreme game of chance – but at
least, collectively, they ensure that the British Royal
House is the oldest of Europe's surviving dynasties.

The role of a hereditary monarch within an unwritten
constitution puzzles outside observers. The Queen cannot
by herself carry out any action of government. She does
however possess freedom of choice in selecting a Prime

Minister to form a government. In 1957 she selected
Harold Macmillan to succeed Sir Anthony Eden, even
though there was a sentiment among some Conservatives
which favoured R. A. Butler. The Queen took the
advice of her private secretariat, and of the Conservative
elder statesmen, before summoning Macmillan to the
palace. In 1963 Elizabeth tacitly amended the constitutional
decision of her grandfather, George V, forty years before,
when he selected Baldwin rather than Curzon. An act of
Parliament, passed in July 1963, permitted peers to
disclaim their peerages for life. Two and a half months
later ill health forced Macmillan to resign and the Queen,
again after extensive consultations, chose as his successor
the Earl of Home who disclaimed his peerage and, as
Sir Alec Douglas-Home, found a 'safe' constituency
and led the Conservative government. Since 1965 all
three main political parties have come to elect their leaders,
a procedure which, it has been argued, will in future limit
the Queen's choice. But this would not be so if there were
a serious rift in the majority party, nor if it became
desirable to form a coalition.

Basically the Queen retains the three prerogatives defined
by Bagehot a few months before Disraeli became Prime
Minister for the first time – 'the right to be consulted, the
right to encourage, and the right to warn'. This is no empty
formula. It governed the important relationship between
George VI and Churchill during the war and it would form
a basis for the functions of the crown should there be a
future radical government of the left or the right. A King
or Queen of Great Britain is always something more than
a representative functionary, but never an initiator of
political change or experiment.

Acknowledgements

The illustrations in this book appear by kind permission of the following. (Sources in brackets refer to picture sources. Sources without brackets are owners).

Aerofilms Ltd, 33 (right); Tom Annan, 107 (top left); James Austin 32 (top right); Cecil Beaton, 146; Bibliotheque Nationale Paris, 18 (bottom), 32 (top left), 32 (centre right), 35, 46 (top); 53 (top), 53 (bottom); Birmingham Public Libraries; Boulton and Watt Collection III (top left): Bodleian Library, Oxford, 63 (left); British Museum, 10, 11, 14 (right), 17, 18 (top), 21, 22, 23, 24, 25, 28, 29, 30, 31, 32 (bottom right), 34, 40, 41, 42, 44 (top right, bottom left, bottom right), 45 (left), 46 (bottom), 48 (top), 49, 52 (both), 54, 56, 57, 58, 60, 62 (both), 63 (right), 64, 65, 68, 69 (left), 72, 78, 81 (top centre), 83 (bottom left, bottom right), 85, 89 (top), 92, 95, 96, 98 (top left, top centre, top right, centre, centre right, bottom centre left), 99 (right), 101 (both), 102, 105 (bottom), 106, 109, 111 (top right, centre top, bottom right), 113, 114, 116-7 (top), 118, 125 (top), 131 (right); Duke of Buccleuch and Queensberry (Victoria and Albert Museum), 79 (bottom); (Royal Academy) 84; By Gracious Permission of Her Majesty The Queen, 75 (bottom left), 91, 100, 107 (top right), 116 (bottom), 119, 126, 128, 133, 147 (top); By courtesy of the Dean and Chapter of Canterbury Cathedral, 38, 71; Cambridge University Collection, 45 (right), Camera Press, 136, 152-3 (Patrick Lichfield); Chequers, 98 (top centre left); Courtauld Institute of Art, 13; Department of the Environment, 20, 122 (bottom); Fine Art Photography, 125 (bottom); John Frost World Wide Newspaper Collectors Club, 135; Gloucester Cathedral (A. F. Kersting), 50; Guildhall Library, 143 (bottom); Historical Picture Services, Chicago, 51; Imperial War Museum, 140 (both), 141 (top left, top right, centre left, bottom left); Kenneth Jagger, 67 (top); Earl of Jersey Collection, 81 (centre left); A. F. Kersting, 48 (bottom); Keystone Press Agency, 149 (bottom); Kunsthistorisches Museum Vienna, 75 (centre left); Lambeth Palace Library, by courtesy of His Grace the Archbishop of Canterbury, 55, 67 (bottom); Louvre Paris (Giraudon) 93; Mansell Collection, 105 (top); Master and Fellows of St. John's College Cambridge, 73 (right); Lord Methuen, Corsham Court, 81 (bottom right); Metropolitan Museum of Art, New York, Gift of J. P. Morgan 1917, 87; Musee de la Ville de Bayeux (Giraudon), 8; (Victoria and Albert Museum), 16, 19 (top); Musee Jacquemest Arrohe (Bulloz), 27; Museum of London, 129; Lt.Col. R. Myddelton, Chirle Castle, 107 (bottom); National Army Museum, 130 (centre), 131 (left); National Gallery of Scotland, 127; National Gallery, Washington D.C. Samuel H. Kress Collection, 94; National Maritime Museum (Weidenfeld and Nicolson Archives) 124; National Monuments Record, 15 (both). National Portrait Gallery, 19 (bottom), 61, 66, 69 (right), 73 (left), 75 (top right), 75 (top left), 75 (bottom right), 77, 81 (top left), 81 (centre right), 82, 97, 98 (bottom left), 98-9, 121, 130 (bottom left), 130 (bottom right), 135, 138, 144; Photri, USA, 141 (centre right); Pierport Morgan Library, 32 (bottom left); Popperfoto, 12, 141 (bottom right), 147 (bottom), 151 (above), 154; Duke of Portland, 90 (left); Press Association, 139; Public Record Office (Mansell Collection), 14 (left), 83 (top), 86; Royal Institution of Cornwall, 111 (bottom left); Royal Library Windsor, 36; Royal Naval College, Greenwich, 108, 112; Royal Society, 90 (right); Lord Sackville, Knole, 81 (top right); Scala, 76; Science Museum, 110 (left), 111 (centre bottom); Syndication International, 151 (below), 152 (left); Roger Viollet, 9; Walker Art Gallery Liverpool, 74; Weidenfeld and Nicolson Archives, 39, 44 (top left), 80 (left), 115, 143 (top); Simon Wingfield-Digby, Sherborne Castle, 80-81; Endpapers, Phaidon Press.

The author, Weidenfeld and Nicolson, and Octopus have taken all possible care to trace and acknowledge the source of all illustrations reproduced in this book. If any errors have occurred the publishers will be pleased to correct them in further editions, provided that they receive notification.

PDO 79-314